# The Seasoned Woman Speaks

of living graciously with substance

Life is a gift. Accept it.

by

## Dr. Theda Palmer

The Seasoned Woman, Inc.
Park West Finance Station
P.O. Box 20616
New York, New York 10025

# Table of Contents

# Introduction by Lydia Ann Haley

Around the fall of 1993, my brother, Bill Haley, introduced me to a woman who, little did I know at the time, would have a major impact on my life. We met at a time when my life was turned inside out. My dad, the writer Alex Haley, had passed on in 1992. His death triggered an unraveling that not only affected my life, but other family members as well.

I found myself at the crossroads and for the first time in my life, I didn't have a solution at hand. There was no one there for me. I felt betrayed by friends — many of whom, I was shocked to discover, only dealt with me because of my father's fame.

In walked Theda Palmer, bringing into my life her witty, acerbic and efficient way of handling what needed to be done. Her attitude was, "OK, what's done is done. Let's move forward." She helped me to recover my self-esteem at a time when I felt my bare ass was exposed for the world to see. She was truly an angel in disguise.

Theda comes from a long line of unusual Black women who define the nature of a culture. Her experience is one of giving, of commitment and perseverance in the finest traditions of our ancestors. Her evolution as a creation of God — as a woman — is an inspiration to the modern woman.

You will enjoy these "recipes of life." They are straightforward, candid and very helpful. This lady is not afraid to step forward and lend a helping hand to those who need guidance.

*Lydia, the daughter of the late Alex Haley,*
*lives in North Carolina with her mother Nanny Haley.*

# Dedication

To the outstanding Seasoned Women in my family:

My grandmothers, Carrie and Dovie; my mother, Pauline and my sister Paulette.

To the almost Seasoned Women:

My nieces, Maya and Jolaine.

Published by
The Seasoned Woman, Inc.
Park West Finance Station
P.O. Box 20616
New York, New York 10025 USA
Library of Congress Control #2002095837
ISBN: 0-9724216-0-2
Printed in New York City, New York

Revised 2003
The data were collected from women in communication groups and
individually, over a ten-year period. The material, presented as life
recipes, concerns issues relevant to women age 50 and above. A
discussion guide follows each life recipe to encourage further
communication.

This book is available in quantity discounts and individual
purchases at select bookstores, on the Internet and through the
publisher SW, Inc.

For information, e-mail: Swoman4@juno.com or fax
212.666.7382

# Acknowledgements

Nothing happens without the blessing of the master planner — God. I owe all to the grace of God.

I thank my family — the Palmer and Washington clan — for unconditional love and support throughout my life. They are my protection and motivation.

This adventure that became a book is due to the faith and efforts of my extended family and friends whom I hear acknowledge: to Sheila Thorne for inspiration; Larry Houston, John Purvis, Ruthie Browning Wynn and Gladys Lee, Clarence Willis and Liv Wright, who gave encouragement and support to complete my work. Thank you for your time. Christine Strong Cacey I am forever grateful to you for putting my words into proper form.

Monika Webb and Bill Griffin cleaned up the technical bugs with ease and made my writing less stressful from the first printed word to the last. You made the book possible. Also, I'm blessed to have received the many benefits provided by Leroy Williams that helped make my writing environment ideal.

My recent marriage to Bill Saxton gave me the best gifts of all — time and independence. Because of his generosity and emotional support, I had the luxury of being a full-time writer and an independent publisher.

# Foreword
## Getting My Flavor

The kitchen table at our flat in St. Louis was the center for nourishing the body, mind and spirit. Young and old had a place there, but wisdom and experience, for the most part, had the leadership role in shaping the mold that would direct the design of the "life recipes" used. The best recipes were kept and reworked from generation to generation. We kept them alive in the family by using them in countless "living stews."

A living stew is not a neat and easy preparation. Nor is it economical. Its composition demands variety and planning. The good stew has ingredients that are based on availability and logical sequence. Seasoning happens in layers upon layers of blended spices and herbs. It's a slow process. A stew has distinct properties that are recognizable by taste and form, and blends into a unifying sauce full of aromatic flavor. It requires work.

Our kitchen table could cook up a recipe for a family member's personal "living stew" that was dependable. We concocted recipes while trying to live out our unique "stews" as we went about our daily lives. Some of us found ourselves in stews more frequently than other family members, but the solutions were always offered for guidance and support.

Our family practice of coming together is a practice that I associate with detailed food preparation and joyful consumption. We love the whole labor-intensive process. My most cherished memories are grounded in our traditions of sharing food and celebrating each other's lives, in good and bad times. Aging has taught me to respect our organized system of creating an accessible network. It is there for us to dip into for knowledge and inspiration.

I miss being at the table when it's time to put together a recipe for coping with a problem on the school bus with an 8-year-old niece or nephew, missed homework assignments from the family teens, unemployment and mortgage payments to be kept up, expenses for college tuition, illness and homecare for our elders, misunderstandings between parents and their adult children, dissolution of home life brought on by separation and divorce, the celebration of births and deaths, and the allocation of property. Most of all, I miss the pressing of the flesh, the touching that accompanied the honest and loving contributions to flavor my pot, that was sincerely motivated to prepare for me a whole and happy stew. This is the basis of the landscape from where I view the world.

Putting together conversations I've had with women over the years has inspired me to offer the recipe "living stew format" to others, in hopes they will add perspective to their daily trials of life. Passing on the information communicated by other cooks who have "been there and done that" is a way to make a modern day "life stew" in a world replete with obstacles and messy complications.

The Seasoned Woman Speaks reveals ways in which we can become more connected to each other and use our seasoning to influence world opinion on living humanely. The transforming healing power to solve problems using culturally customized recipes, designed at the kitchen tables around the world, is more powerful than artificial beauty, computer-generated relationships, money-driven status symbols and egotistical, power-stricken politicians.

Seasoned Women can cook up a delicious stew to address real people issues and they can make the need for violent confrontation of the spirit, mind and body pointless. Healthy recipes, replicated by world-class cooks, leave me comfortable in my "St. Louis-kitchen-table state of mind."

Take charge and cook your own stew because life will, if you don't.

Enjoy the feast.


Theda

A Seasoned Woman

# In Our Own Image

Necessity is the mother of invention. It is necessary for maturing women to create their own images. We must own the paintbrush that paints the picture the world uses to define who we are. We must take charge of the image the world responds to where a woman over age 50 is concerned.

In the past, we had the task of redefining the context of our lives, as it applied to unjust laws governing our nation. Our age group forced the sexist, patriarchal white male to change policies designed to exclude minorities and women. Unfortunately, we declared success too soon.

Age discrimination was legally attacked as an employment and benefits issue. It was necessary for the laws governing aging employees to change. Significant changes in laws governing aging employees had to change to accommodate increased longevity.

As a result, the senior executive is currently viewed as a valuable asset for corporations. Contrastingly, the image of the aging woman still carries a stigma that no amount of legislation has relieved.

## Changing Imagery

During the battle for civil rights, certain rights specific to aging women were not even considered. The gains that were made which echoed afterward, in the form of the feminist movement, applied to younger women. Unfortunately, a false image of a huge part of society was left unchanged.

Demographically, Baby Boomers are thought of in the past tense. In fact, we energetically participate in every facet of life. Moreover, we are capable of painting truer portraits of ourselves than the purveyors of target groups. The woman in the mirror can speak for us.

The term "Seasoned Women" expresses what we are and how we came to be what we are. The years have made us better. The drippings from our essence flavor the stew of life. A Seasoned Woman cannot be conceptualized as the old stereotype from years past.

Stereotypes were never kind and totally incompatible with contemporary women blessed with longevity. They only served to cloak mature women in a cloud of shame for having the nerve to live beyond age 40. Let us be clear, longevity is not a curse.

Longevity is God's gift to you. God's graciousness chose you to survive the hills and valleys of life. Your blessed, durable body holds the treasure within.

As vital women who have been so blessed, we must value ourselves by using language that promotes positive imagery and provides uplift. We must stop participating in counterproductive verbal attacks on ourselves and stop allowing ourselves to be the butt of jokes. While maintaining a healthy sense of humor about the divine comedy that is life, speak of yourself as a rare treasure. Always communicate your seasoned womanhood in terms of the present.

I am a Seasoned Woman; I am at ease with myself. My graying, thinning hair, the blueness of my varicose veins, the dimples of my cellulite, the lines in my face and the furrow of my brow all came through years, days and minutes of my life spent trying to stay alive. I celebrate birthdays and long life. I celebrate living.

There are approximately 33 million Seasoned Women; whereas, there are only 27 million seasoned men. As a group, we can change how America functions politically and economically by the sheer numbers and amount of wealth that comes from our pockets. We're the most powerful segment of the population and we're still growing.

Our image is out of touch with the real picture because we have not assumed a leadership role in asserting our true womanhood.

Once she perceives herself as a rare blend of herbal combinations, the Seasoned Woman will embrace the remnants left from pain, joy and sorrow. We are living testimonies to the effects of successes, failures, and of proud and embarrassing moments. We have made and lost friends. We have made love and been left lonely, and we have rejoiced and cursed the sunrises and sunsets of our lives.

When the Seasoned Woman thinks about all that it has taken to grace each stepping-stone, how can she apologize for herself? How can she want to excuse her appearance? How can she want to obliterate her reality because men have convinced her that she is no longer a vibrant woman? How can women permit men to assign to them characteristics that have nothing to do with their past, present or future well being? Women with positive, clear self-concepts do not want to weigh less than skinny, 14-year-old girls. Unfortunately, this is the visual picture that is pumped out as beauty.

## Unloading Unhealthy Baggage

Our self-perceptions are influenced by the bombardment of advertisers. We are not immune to the seduction of television, radio and other media. However, we need to detoxify our systems from the poison spread through advertising that fosters self-hatred for the aging process. Aging men, on the other hand, are marketed differently.

Mostly controlled by men, marketing campaigns primarily show aging men as healthy and eminently masculine. The energy of their positive presentation captures the sexual attention of both men and women.

When an aging man has a large belly, baldhead and lines in his face, he is considered mature and sophisticated. He is considered powerful. He is allowed to pursue women that are the age of his daughter. Even though his aging prostate may be engulfing his swelling groin, he is portrayed as having limitless sexual vitality.

On the other hand, marketers use menopause to write off half the female population. It is an automatic disclaimer to vibrant womanhood. The image-makers' failure to show aging women in the same sexually exciting contexts as men of the same age pushes us into the darkness, if we're willing to go. The overworked image of women suffering because of menopause is never far from our consciousness.

Consciously or not, women are set up to dread aging. It is easy to write off a population that expects to have a future filled with emotional turmoil and depression. It is hard to imagine, but some women contribute to their own debasement by referring to menopause as the "change of life." What do you change into? It suggests that you're no longer the same person. Think about yourself before you speak about yourself.

Aging men are who they are into midlife. They maintain a high opinion of themselves and don't change into anything.

# Self-Appreciation

I take my position as a Seasoned Woman seriously and as such, I attract people.

I am a mentor, a friend and I am appreciated as a woman who shares wisdom in solving problems in the workplace and in intimate relationships. Also, I often mediate within troubled families.

Families are fragile, today. People are fragile. Fathers, mothers and children are distant from each other, geographically and spiritually.

Frequently, love is expressed by giving expensive gifts. True love is time sacrificed in large and small ways, time that smoothes over rough places. Love is closeness. Love is an active verb that demands contact. Families need to be close to stay connected to a loving spirit.

Family love is like getting to turn the handle of the ice cream maker at a family picnic. You watch the ice and the rock salt mix around the container as you crank the handle. It seems like forever and when the handle cannot make another turn, you know it's ready.

Everybody comes running. When the top is opened and the smooth ice cream is dipped out, you remember the struggle. You remember what it took to get to that sweet, smooth ice cream.

The loving thing that my mother, a Well Seasoned Woman, says to me as I leave for the airport after a St. Louis visit is, "You stay in touch." She reminds me how important I am in the circle of family love.

My formal education in communications is now grounded in practical experience. Now that I have aged, my education makes more sense. I can use information as an active tool.

I am not dismayed when parts of society push me aside because of my age. Other people reach out to me for assistance.

One of the privileges of getting older is being able to carefully select how and with whom I spend my time. I have options. I finally can spend time doing what I love to do. I'm thrilled to serve as a life coach and mentor for others to resolve conflict. So, I respond to my seasoning with the joy of sharing God's gifts.

It is my hope that women will begin to see themselves as gifted, Seasoned Women. We must take charge and shape seasoned images for ourselves that permit us to feel at ease. Imagine 33 million empowered women using their wisdom to improve the quality of life for everyone. That's what seasoned women can do.

We are here for a purpose and we are what we do. Longevity is not an accident or a mistake. Our long lives will be viewed with respect when we push the envelope.

God did not define you in an advertising campaign. You don't need validation. You have lived more than half a century. At this point in your life, you can live your purpose. Open the gift that is you and use it.

In case you were saving it for old age, well it's here. Now, get off your rusty dusty and get busy!

# Recipe for the Seasoned Woman

Mix torrents of air and light in the universal pot
until water appears.
Its mass will take on a form foreign, but familiar.
Heat it slowly under a spell of moonlight's glow.
Then let it stand, untouched and unnamed
until the need to know, to hold,
to care which cross it needs
to bear is necessary.
The likeness of warm spring breezes,
snowflakes and peach fuzz
left afloat by the mammoth's winged nonstop ocean voyage
to a predetermined destination
is now so compelling,
so urgent that its course has to be.

It suckles innocently on the prickled crown thorns,
with ravenous appetite.
Bleeding. Feasting.
Equal to no others in flight,
in a way uncanny, unexplored until
inertia gives it sight.

To this miraculous vessel of perfectly shaped air,
gliding upon foam-capped crests with such clarity
of light
based on faith, not in need of sight
to see the unthinkable journey
beneath the feet of life not yet imprinted by ignorance
and hate,
comes hope.

Settling down spread-eagle onto a space of level flatness
for all to partake
and fill their empty caverns of
bottomless bellies of the night in search of air,
light and water
in the form of the familiar.

Searching for the connection between the destination
and its purpose,
the hunger needs and seeks a natural place
to feed, to grow
and learn to know
this breath of living air.

Miraculously formed of rare stock, she flows
forth in full light of day
unapologetically naked
to the world,
dressed in undeniable intelligence and grace.

She lays on hands of healing balm
to hold away pain and miseries promised
to the overstuffed bellies of greed and need.
Both, equally insatiable.
Each, equally selfish.

For they will always be in need of something
beyond their capacity to get,
to hold onto,
to depend on and
go peacefully into sleep.

With compassion for and wisdom of
life's endless hunger,
the Seasoned Woman provides and satisfies.

# Kicking the Recipe Around the Table
## In Your Own Image

1. What language do you use to describe yourself as an aging woman?

2. Are you ever bothered by the general attitudes of society towards the mature population?

3. Does the term "senior citizen" describe how you see yourself?

4. Will your life change significantly because of your new, aging status?

5. How do you explain the concept that "the best is yet to come"?

6. What activities no longer receive the large amount of time they once did? Why?

# "Wake Up and Smell the Coffee"

There is the possibility of getting confused about your age, when you think you're getting older. But trust me, the appearance of your first gray pubic hair eliminates the confusion. The fact of getting older is clear when the hair covering your vagina starts turning gray. It is far more dramatic than seeing silver strands while combing your hair. Neither is welcomed.

You expect to have gray hair on your head, eventually. You see women and men with gray hair all the time. But pubic hair is a private hair story. The only thing worse is pubic hair loss.

The balding vagina gets no discussion whatsoever. It's not even a private conversation with your best girlfriend; it's too real. Denial works better than tweezers for a while.

Dark and Lovely and Clairol promote wide ranges of colors for aging tresses, from the sides of buses, in magazines, on billboards and television. But you're on your own with your pubic hair situation. Your pubic revolution will not be televised. The hair care industry has no way to cover up or restore thinning pubic hair, yet. Possibly, it never will.

Needless to say, this particular rite-of-passage gets your attention. Aging happens in small, day-to-day discoveries, like the skin loosening on your face, arms and hands.

Body changes appear without fanfare, as if delivered by a ghost. However, the appearance of gray pubic hair creates havoc because it is where you and your lover touch.

Based on conversations I initiated with women concerning the aging process, the changed appearance of the vaginal area is the most difficult to accept.

The majority felt that it signaled lessened sexual capability. With less pussy power (P-power), they feared their lovers would be turned off. Decreased P-power was a major concern for both single and married heterosexual women. Many felt that their enjoyment of receiving oral sex would be compromised, if they were anxious about their appearance.

With genital baldness as an option, an amazing number of unmarried women were unconcerned about the absence of hair or the presence of pain. They confessed to yanking out gray pubic hair with tweezers. Others did extensive hair removal by getting a hair wax.

After a time using these desperate measures, these women surrender the fight against nature and leave the graying process to run its course.

One evening after work, I stopped by a benefit for an organization of retired local athletes. I considered them peers, older men I could enjoy at parties and other affairs.

Once inside the club and finished with the greeting hugs and kisses, I went to the bar, ordered my usual spring water — no ice with a twist of lime. The music was great and I sat near the dance area and relaxed. I had worked a hard day and sitting quietly, undisturbed was welcomed.

After an hour or so, I moved to a table closer to the dance floor. I was ready to socialize and dance. I sat and waited and waited. Not one man came to me. They smiled and walked on by.

Shocked, I watched men between 50 and 65 years old competing with 30-year-old men for the attention of younger women. Watching older men fumbling for business cards and trying to write phone numbers without the benefit of their thick eyeglasses was hilarious.

Then I remembered how I had once been the younger woman in demand. I had watched older women waiting for invitations to dance that never came as I worked it on the dance floor, in my short black dress.

Armed with the latest dance steps, I partied through almost three decades. Being a petite-size probably accounted for the long period of time that I captured the attention of men who partied with the hope of getting over.

The male's fun is in the chase. The female ego booster is being chased, whether welcomed or not. It was P-power that created the testosterone frenzies.

But now, the movie script had flipped. I was reduced to an indignant wallflower. How could I wait passively for the Electric Slide to play, so that I could leave feeling as though I had danced at least once? After an hour of sitting, I ate the bitter slice of lime, drank the bitter water and left.

I entered the club still thinking I was the woman of years before. In my mind, I was still Miss Party Thing who still had it going on. I didn't know I was wearing my mother's shoes. No pop-up sign appears to say, "Wake up girl! You're 50!"

When I left the club feeling semi-crushed, it was still early. It was an abnormally warm New York City evening, in the middle of winter. The weather displaced some of the lingering bad taste left over from the club. The night air enthralled me.

Walking the street and enjoying the warm breeze was conducive to a little quick shopping. The unpredictable weather was the kind that could lead to getting a cold if you defied common sense and removed your coat.

After years of listening to my mother's warnings about dressing properly for the weather, I surrendered to the warmth and removed my coat. As I descended the subway stairs on Broadway, I had the feeling that it would be full and it was. Jostling for my regular place on the crowded platform behind the yellow caution line, where the doors to the first car usually open, proved to be the easiest part of my trip home.

Only one side of the two subway doors opened in front of me. This was not a good sign. As the riders filed out past me even more slowly than usual, I could see the two adjacent doors had properly opened, allowing passengers on quickly. By the time I got on, all the available seats were gone. Unless a gentleman stood to give me a seat, it was going to be a stand-on-tired-feet situation. After scanning the subway train, I was sure the men who remained seated had on shoes more comfortable than mine.

I was unaware that my red coat had been swinging from my shoulder like a crimson cape. Its chic belt was stuck in the subway door. The train could not move.

I tried to pull the coat to free the belt, but not before the conductor's voice bellowed over the public address system, "Would the passenger decorating my train with the lovely red belt please remove it from the door, so my train can move!"

Ignoring the mean stares, I yanked hard and freed my belt. In a moment, we were on our way. With the typical straphanger's blank expression, I let my line of vision stray as far away from my red coat as possible. Privately, I said, "You're right, Mom. I should've kept the coat on."

My roving eyes took in newspapers, backpacks and bobbing heads wearing headphones. My eyes were suddenly drawn to a man sitting on the opposite side of the packed train. He was doing the unthinkable; he was making eye contact. I figured he had to be from out of town. If he wasn't, he had to be a pervert of some kind.

Instinctively, I retreated into a blank stare to shield myself from his intrusive glare. But during the brief eye contact, I saw that he was not bad to look at. In a woman's way of quickly taking in things, I saw he had a certain GQ flare. His deep-set, soft brown eyes perfectly suited his close haircut and he wore no earrings. Other than that, I couldn't identify him in a police line up.

I shifted my attention to my shopping bags and the coat that I held close to me out of the way of the subway doors. Without looking at the man, I could feel him checking me out.

Now, if my hot-flash sweat glands continued to cooperate, I had a chance of escaping the train and the flirtatious stranger without a red face.

My stop was coming up next.

Getting off with the crush of passengers pushing through the one functioning door was almost as traumatic as getting on. But I managed to get off without another public address announcement. A nearby bench gave me a brief moment to myself. Belatedly, I put on my coat.

The suction of air from the departing train created a back-draft. As my coat flared from the underground breeze, a guiding hand from behind assisted my arm into my sleeve. Looking back, I saw a man smiling as he gently pulled my coat up evenly onto my shoulders and turned down the collar around the back of my neck. With a casual ease, he had me into my coat.

He brushed my braids back and smoothed my lapel. The warmth generated by his subtle but aggressive manner, combined with his respectful touch on the back of my neck, ignited a hot wave of forgotten lust.

I found myself wishing the cotton lining of my bikini panties was a dam when I began to get moist. I pretended not to feel the heat coming from my clinching buttocks.

Inwardly, I was embarrassed, but I was taken by the spontaneity of the moment. Anticipating our first eye contact, when I turned to face him, was almost too much to bear.

I turned to look at him. I was not disappointed. My attention span was divided between his full, smiling lips framed by a well-manicured mustache, with flecks of gray hair and the throng of people rushing past us at the subway stop.

His voice was as manly as he was handsome when he said,

"Let me help you with those bags."

I only smiled, to hold on to mystery.

He said, "I tried to get your attention on the train. I was going to offer you my seat."

Without my OK, he reached for my bags. I said, "Oh, don't bother. I can handle it."

Then, he said something that startled me. "It's been a long time. How've you been?"

I can't imagine the look on my face, but my mind raced like a computer retrieving files of information to place this man in some context of my life.

I cursed my unoriginal question, hearing myself ask, "Do I know you from someplace?"

"Careful where you step; my ego's down there. I'm Taylor Martin."

I was still clueless. Then he dropped the bomb, loudly.

"You taught me drama in the 11th grade!"

The words resounded as a part of me wanted to fall down next to his ego and die, but I remained on my feet.

Taylor may have been my student, but he never majored in women because he had no inkling how mortified I was. He barreled on.

"It was your first year teaching. Remember? You were so pretty and young. After school, I used to paint theatre sets just to be around you."

Taylor took me back twenty-nine years to Spanish Harlem. I was a green, 22-year-old teacher with tough 17- and 18-year-old students who had no use for a system that had no use for them.

Sure, I remembered. How could I forget the education they dished out to me with a giant spoon?

My breath was shallow. My heart was pounding and my mouth was drier than the Sahara. I felt the moisture in my panties mingle with my pubic hair. I twitched in discomfort.

Taylor said, "I never missed a class. I started to read and concentrate because of you and those plays. I'll always remember you."

My brain was trying to switch gears. As I looked into Taylor Martin's face, a vague feeling of familiarity came over me.

His words smashed me like a sledgehammer. A familiar lust rushed over me like the wind from an oncoming train.

"You look a little faint," Taylor said. "Sure you don't need help?

I mumbled something I hoped was a response. He took out his business card and gave it to me. He extended his hand and engulfed my damp palm.

"I just closed on a loan for a small building uptown for my media production business. Now, meeting you on the same day is a sign I'm still on a winning streak."

All I could do was smile as Taylor pulled high school memories out of long ago. The accuracy of his memory was scarily impeccable.

My former 17-year-old student, Taylor Martin, had grown into a hunky 46-year-old man.

With a soft rub of my shoulder and a gentle kiss on my cheek, Taylor walked down the platform and disappeared into the crowd. Holding on to his business card, I remained motionless.

My face was beginning to flush. Sweat poured from my hairline. It felt like a hot, slow leak. There was a matching flow around my breast and down my neck. As I fumbled for a tissue, I looked back at the empty bench. I had the feeling something was left behind.

Emerging from the staircase leading to the street was a monumental task. My legs felt too thick to be balanced on the high-heeled leather pumps. My lungs hungrily sucked in the crisp, cool evening air.

The short walk home became more pleasurable with each step. My walk fell into a rhythm. City noise became endearing sounds. The scintillating smell of food from a restaurant enticed my nose.

I was getting hungry and couldn't wait to eat and see Selbra. She was my mentor and shoulder to lean on, and I was her sounding board. We had a reciprocal relationship. Selbra and I treated each other with compassion and respect.

Fortunately, Selbra was up. We called out for food, went to the kitchen table where I drank hot tea. Selbra waited for me to justify my spontaneous weeknight visit. Struggling for words that wouldn't come was new for me.

Suddenly, I felt insecure. Selbra was patient with me. When the floodgates opened, I cried as much as I talked. As I talked, I was afraid of what she would tell me I was becoming. She knew me so well.

Over a generous mound of cherry cheesecake, she waited for me to finish unraveling the ball tying me up. While Selbra waited, she told me things I already knew, but needed to hear echoing from a friend. She heard me recount my disappointment about not being asked to dance at the club and how Taylor Martin cruelly reminded me of how young I wasn't anymore.

Through the night, Selbra and I talked through the years, until late night became the early day. The conversation we shared led me to a peaceful place within myself.

Advice from women always inspired me. It was like how I felt when my mother explained menstruation to my sister, Paulette and me. She told us to expect body changes: we would grow breasts, and hair under our arms and between our legs; we would release blood, monthly.

Our mother, Pauline, told us to anticipate excitement, thinking about boys and cautioned that sexual intercourse would make us pregnant. I still remember the mother/daughter film my mother showed on our living room wall, projected onto a sheet. Many of the girls on our block learned the reality of childbirth from Pauline.

While growing from childhood into puberty, my sister, Paulette and I were given a great deal of counseling by our mother. Unfortunately, home is over 1,000 miles away at this stage of my continuing development.

I had needed a bridge, not a clock turned back. I'm blessed to have a friend like Selbra to sensitively give me my wake-up call. Not every woman does.

Age groups, unlike the voluntary membership in social organizations, cannot be orchestrated. Age groupings are set in motion at birth and proceed in a natural sequence for as long as you are alive. But age-appropriate behavior is uniquely individual.

Acting your age, whatever that means, has become more difficult to identify in contemporary society. Individuals age 50 and over run their own companies, have new careers after retirement and have children later in life, more than ever before.

After my subway encounter with Taylor and my mentoring session with Selbra, I realized that I was not alone. Many women over 50, whom I know and others whom I never met, are going through their own reckoning with the notion of no longer being the young, fly girl in popular demand.

Upon investigation, I was surprised at how unique each woman is who responded to my inquiries. A primary question was how they accepted getting older. I was keenly interested in their reactions to their personal wake-up calls from Mother Time.

I was impressed at their willingness to offer themselves as mentors and share wisdom with younger women. They are seasoned in a variety of spices and will provide leadership for generations to come. Hear them as they speak:

# Doris Brunson

"My personal wake-up call, reminding me that I was older, came gradually over a period of time as policemen, store clerks, bus drivers and teenagers began to refer to me as ma'am. I realized that the old face was rapidly catching up with my (no longer) prematurely gray hair."

### Doris' Recipe:

"My greatest pleasure in maturing is being alive during such a challenging period of history. I feel that I have a place now where I can stand and look back at the past, experience the present and plan for a future.

"I struggle with my thoughts of the past because some of its softer memories reach out to hold me in place with reminders of the spiritual closeness of long-lost family and friends, our love of learning, music, art and the impeccable manners which made life so much sweeter.

"As I think about all of the marvelous achievements of great educators, musicians, artists, athletes, dramatists, actors, architects and doctors of the past, I feel happy to have been a witness to such momentous and creative events.

"Of course from my vantage point, I am forced to experience the pain of the present, for it is marred by the ugly racism of the past. If I have any unhappiness about aging, it is knowing that our nation will never accept Black people on an equal basis despite the fact that we have risen to the top of any field of endeavor which has been opened to us. I have a fierce pride in and love for my people because they have achieved on levels that few others could have done given the depth and breadth of the obstacles placed before them.

"The remarkable thing is that even though some of us have buckled under the strain of the day-to-day onslaught of overt and subtle racism, most have moved ahead with knowledge borne of educational struggle, mother wit borne of the soul and humor borne of the heart.

"My main sadness is that our country has never understood that we could be light-years ahead of all other nations in terms of spiritual, cultural, social, political and economic development if people of color, whether or not they are nationals or immigrants, were allowed to participate in the American dream to their fullest capabilities.

"We have a great country despite its shortcomings, but its greatness seems to be diseased by the selfish, immoral greed of those who care nothing for others. The insidious desire to control people instead of opening opportunities for them to achieve their fullest potential is devastating.

"I am very concerned about our teens. Too many of them have not learned to have respect for the past. Their view seems to be that if it did not happen yesterday, it is not important or valuable. Our schools and responsible adults must share in the task of informing them about past events and their implications for the future. If America is diseased, all of our young people must be the cure.

"I would ask our youth to consider reaching out in their communities where they could join in the demands for more youth services and opportunities, where they could serve others through volunteerism and where they could explore the philosophies, religions and codes of behavior which would guide them safely into their future.

"I would like to advise their parents, including the 35-plus generation of women, to encourage their offspring to seek values of the past such as respect for themselves and others, respect for their heritage and respect for the work ethic. Young women must help to provide their children with a more spiritual approach to life in which they are guided by the principles of a God-inspired belief or religion."

## Billie Jean Johnson

"My wake-up call came when my hair began to change colors before my eyes. My knees began to ache; my arms are much weaker now and my gait much slower.

"How had I not noticed that the sun had changed her sundress to an evening gown, full of color and grandeur?

"For now, I understand the most beautiful part of the day, in fact the most beautiful part of a woman's life, is at the setting of the sun.

"All of life's tragedy has been wrestled to the mat, but I still stand to attest the authenticity of my goals, dreams and ambitions."

"While the earth remaineth, seed time and harvest, and cold and heat, and summer and winter and day and night shall not cease."   (Genesis 8:22)

### Billie Jean's Recipe:

"My pleasure has been understanding my role as a mentor. Making available my mentor's personal strengths, resources, network (friendships/contacts) to help a protégé reach his or her goals.

"To teach the younger women again that a reference to youth connotes freshness or what is new.

"Equipping women; training women to live Godly lives. Each one, mentor to one. To be able to influence and strengthen the next generation is bringing me the greatest joy and happiness in my life.

"At one time, I became afraid of not being needed. Looked at aging as not being Prime. The best cut, the highest rate, the best years. Prime means energy, strength and ideas. In our culture, teens think you've lost it if you are over thirty. I began to believe they were right when I found myself peering into the refrigerator and couldn't remember why I opened the door.

"The glory of young men is their strength, gray hair the splendor of the old." (Proverbs 20:29)

"I have serious concerns about children raising themselves. With no direction blunting their future, their brain cells with substance abuse, they have a sense of entitlement. Sold out on name brands.

"Parents must teach children to talk to God and build a personal relationship with him. The home must provide vital, living examples.

"Effective ways are having family time, communicating with one another, encouraging one another and praying together. Engage in discussion and ways to apply Christian principles to life's everyday circumstances. Our children must learn to stay focused. They are important to our future generations. They must stop dying and live.

"Be strong and encouraging to your children; they can achieve any and everything they put their minds to. We need structure in our homes with God being the head of our homes. Women stand and are stable when crisis occurs. Be consistent in all your relationships. One sure way is to have a balanced relationship with God. Don't be afraid or embarrassed to counsel with family/friends. Seek help. As women, we all have some valuable experiences to pass on.

"Finally, as I view the future from my vantage point, I look forward to the privilege of enjoying that which is good in life. I am still delighted to be a Black woman like my strong mother, who admired and valued the courage and strength of Black men like my father.

"I shall follow their example of standing with people of good will in all races to foster equality and beauty wherever I go. Even though there are cruel forces in our world, I feel protected by God and my ancestors. I have learned that the meaning of life is found in the struggle to live. When I leave this world, I pray that I go out of it wanting to live. In that way, I shall be able to show God my appreciation for his greatest gift to me — life!!"

## Vernetta Nelson

"My wake-up to aging was my body's inability to recover from simple cold's fatigue and the realization that these are my 'golden years.'

"My pleasure is the wisdom I am acquiring. My unhappiness is that opportunities are plentiful and I am unable to take advantage of them all.

"If I were younger, I could."

### Vernetta's Recipe:
"My advice to younger people is to look at life as a business."

## Candy Richardson

"My first 'wake-up call' was not a specific incident that took place, but in a very general manner, men just stop flirting with or hitting on me. Just walking down the street, which had always included some guy saying something. One day it just stopped."

**Candy's Recipe:**

"My greatest pleasure in maturing is that after all these years, I finally know that I am what I think and not what I eat or look like. My happiness now comes from what I have to give to my friends and family, as a loving and generous human being and not what comes from what I feel someone should be doing for me.

"Also my goals in life have certainly changed from a very monetary status to include one in which I am constantly working on being a better person. My unhappiness about aging is the forgetfulness that I sometimes experience. But, as a good friend often reminds me, don't blame it on aging. You were forgetting things when you were young.

"I have serious concerns for teens, today. Many of them have been neglected by parents who have not taken the time to do the real parenting. It takes time to raise young people and because of this, so many young people are rushed to feel grown and go off to start their own families for all the wrong reasons.

"I would say to these young people: 'wait, smell the coffee, take a chill-pill; you've got choices; don't make the same mistakes I did; you've got your whole life in front of you!' But didn't our parents tell us the same things? So I don't know what I'd say as an overall generalization. I guess I would try to support and encourage them to get as much information as possible and to pray daily for wisdom and understanding.

"To the generation behind us, I would say to some, 'Keep up the good work' and to others, 'never give up.'"

# Audrey June Fields

"I received a wake-up call while browsing in the bookstore on the waterfront in Cape May, New Jersey. I noticed the other adults milling about, strolling on the boardwalk and avoiding a collision with one another. Naturally, it was a hot summer day. Then, the wake-up call came. I picked up a copy of 'My Special Birth Year,' a small bound book, the pages of time, a nostalgia news report, so compact that the headlines stood at attention. I purchased the report and read the news headlines, famous births, price indexes, etc. At that point, I began to think about the fact that I was a part of an older category of mature people.

"This, coupled with several experiences such as fewer invitations to weddings and social functions, more retirements, the obituary column of the newspaper filled with familiar names of friends and associates, gray hair among the strands (of others, not mine), etc., etc., etc. In addition, my family became an empty nest.

"Older, yes, and definitely mature.

"I think that my greatest pleasure in maturing is understanding the process and realizing it is part of life. Age is just an issue that you confront more and more as an older person. However, you can renew and be new over 50."

### Audrey's Recipe:

"In maturing, I feel I have turned my talents into educational successes at home and on the job. Why? As a hard-working and caring person, I have given my best to each of my children, as well as parents and students that have crossed the job threshold. This is fulfilling and gives me pleasure. I feel that I have made a difference!

"I am not unhappy at all about the aging process. I still have good health. My concern is that losing weight requires more exercise. When you are over fifty, you may not feel like exercising that extra ten or twenty minutes.

"Terrible, isn't it? A minority of our young people seem to have misplaced values. The media seem to focus on their lack of value for life. My concern lies in the subjects of teen pregnancy, education, alternatives to violence, AIDS and other sexually transmitted diseases, and their careers.

"What I have to say to teens would fill a book. I have some suggested guidelines for teens:

- Abstinence (you have your whole life ahead)
- Stay in school, go to college, complete a special course of study after high school, enlist in the armed forces
- Dream (be a dream catcher)
- Reach for the stars
- Have goals
- Make the sacrifice to achieve
- Spend fewer hours watching television, try no TV during the week
- Tape your favorite program, wait for the weekend to view it
- Share the program during a family hour
- Pursue your goals, relentlessly
- Learn from others mistakes
- Read more (for example: 'Chicken Soup' or 'The Teenage Soul')
- Be a volunteer, 'give back'
- Get involved in your community
- Teach others about the gift that keeps giving — recycle
- Say no to drugs and alcohol

"Teens must remember that IF THEY GO THE EXTRA MILE, THEY WILL MAKE PROGRESS. Answer the question, 'What is life?'

"My advice to the 35-plus-year-old women: don't take a droll approach; be aggressive; be convincing; be a risk-taker (you have 35 years of experience). Reach one of your high points before the age of 40. Then, set a new direction: goals for 50. Stay busy.

"If you travel your road, the right road for you, something positive will happen.

"Know that you are attractive, intelligent, insightful and knowledgeable.

"I humbly hope that each Seasoned Woman will let go as you attempt to hold the flurries of snow in an open hand."

## Barbara Lang

"What got my attention about turning 50 was the bombardment of material from AARP. At first, I tossed it all in File 13, as I didn't want to face the fact that I was nearing half a century.

- My pleasure? Much, much wiser; experience has been a good teacher.
- My unhappiness? Constant feeling that I am running out of time. I have a lot left that I wanted to do (both personally and professionally) and I feel that the clock is ticking away."

### Barbara's Recipe:
"Teens/What would I say?
"Concern that they are selling themselves short and many feel

that they do not have a future. Don't let anyone steal your dream before making decisions because we do have choices in our lives.

"Advice to those 35 years plus?

"Take personal time for yourselves. Eat healthy, meditate, exercise daily (it helps to clear the cobwebs).

"The 35-plus-year-old woman needs to be willing to try new things, get new interests. I think many of the 35-plus group are very busy, involved with family, jobs, school work and outside activities that their children are involved in, and house work. It uses up much of their time. It doesn't leave much time for relaxation.

"Be willing to cultivate good friendships. Carve out some time for yourself while working on your career. Because your children will soon be in college and away from home, then you will have more time for interests. There are many more career opportunities, today.

"Women can accomplish whatever they wish. Try to have fun. Life passes much too fast."

## Althea Giles

"I have no frame of reference to a wake-up call as an indicator that I am in an older category. My life has moved along very methodically. I still do many of the same things I did as a younger woman such as 50 sit-ups a day. I still love to dance. I still work in sales, meeting and talking to new people. I still attend many trade shows. I go out on sales calls. I still travel. Many people are quite surprised at my youthful appearance.

"My greatest pleasure in maturing is seeing the many changes in the world. A feeling that I have passed each stage in life with satisfaction, happiness, peace and accomplishment.

Many strides have been made in science and medicine. There are new things to learn each day. I find myself able to take advantage of the new technology. The world is changing with the advent of the Internet, which brings many new problems. I am happy that I am a mature woman, very much satisfied with my life, but sense that younger women have many mountains to climb. I am mostly upset by man's inhumanity to one another. The caring and friendship of neighbor to neighbor and respect for one another seems to be lost. The fact that racism has reared its ugly head is very troubling.

"I have no unhappiness about aging. I have been well and have unusual vitality and meet each day with resolve and another day to work at the things I find dear to my heart. I love life; life has been fulfilling. My life is filled with fun and many exciting things to do. I have a wonderful, exciting group of friends that I spend a lot of time with in Paris, Spain and around the country.

"All of my friends are exciting accomplished men and women. When we meet, we have challenging conversation and a lot of fun; we laugh a lot, listen to music and enjoy being together. I have also been committed to many causes, which has brought fulfillment and a feeling of satisfaction that I have been able to help my fellow man in some small way. I have received recognition for many of the things that I have done. This brings great satisfaction.

"I have many serious concerns for teens and the many problems that they face every day. They are vulnerable every day that they walk out of the house. It is very difficult to follow a straight and narrow course when many of your friends and peers are involved with drugs and anti-social behavior.

"Many teens have sex at a very early age and are faced with pregnancy. There is explicit sex on TV. Promiscuous sex at an early age increases the danger of AIDS and sexually transmitted disease. Babies are having babies; they have no parental skill or work skills. Many parents are allowing their youngsters to have sex at home. Too often when a new baby is brought into the home, it strains the family resources and increases the cycle of poverty. They never understand the beauty of a loving relationship with meaningful sex.

"There are far too many guns in youngsters' hands; the violence among teens is very disturbing. Drugs are another serious concern. Youngsters are starting to take drugs at a very early age, before they reach their teens. Many go into treatment several times.

"Racism is another serious problem that teens face because we as a race are perceived a criminals with no morals or value systems. Some teens are well adjusted; some of them are excelling in school following rules and are fine citizens. We very rarely hear about the many fine things that many teens are involved in."

**Althea's Recipe:**
"I would say to the teens: Go to school, study and excel. This is a way of changing your life. Say no to drugs and early sex. Spend much of your time in the library reading, excel in sports and spend your time involved with sports events. Respect mom and dad or your parent. They are providing you with your basic needs. They love you very much. Follow the rules of the house. You will soon be a young adult and you can make your own choices.

"Prepare yourself for a job or further education; go to college, business school or trade school. Go to church, involve yourself with the teen programs such as basketball, softball, etc. If you have had a baby while you are very young, you can go back to school, get your education and you will be better able to provide for your family."

## Lillian Pierce

"Haven't noticed aging because it's not a big thing in my life and I have no regrets about it."

### Lillian's Recipe:

"I'd like to remind young people that they should stay in school no matter what and never give up on yourself."

## Valerie Williams

"Living, with me at 54. Where did the time go? The years came so fast. I've done a lot, touched a lot of young people who are now out on their own and successful. I am truly pleased about that. They have come back to tell me about how what I said or did helped them.

"There's a word now that constantly comes into conversation as the novel of life plays out, the word retirement. Am I ready? Yes. What new adventures will I try?

"Going to Puerto Rico for college was an adventure in itself. I learned so much from that experience: a new language, a new culture and lasting friendships. I even worked in the school system before returning to the States. My Peace Corp work was done before the Peace Corp became popular! Learning to fly a plane and scuba dive confirmed the adventure. The Spanish language opened doors for me that might have been closed. I even tried the experience of marriage for a short time. Some adventures are not for everyone.

"Now I notice that fatigue seems to set in too early. Cannot put more than one or two activities in a day. The mind is well, but the body isn't.

"Gray hair and fuller figure.

"Seeing that statistics are right. There are more women than men out in the world.

"Greatest pleasures?

"Being myself and not worrying about what people say or do. Having respect for their style and hope they in turn have respect for mine.

"God, my family, friends, the strength I've gotten from each. Doing nothing and not feeling guilty about it.

"The aging process, it came so fast. Making mature decisions, but not always wanting to be mature.

"People telling me I'm too young to retire. What will I do? Back to school for something else other than the educational field, something just for me!"

**Valerie's Recipe:**

"Many of our teens have had to face too many adult problems, too early in life. Many have missed the real growing process. They must not let the streets win. Even if you have lemons, make lemonade. Learn to turn negative situations into positive forces for the future.

"Enjoy being young. Take each stage as a rite-of-passage. Don't hate your parents/guardians or elders when they give advise or discipline you. Of course, abuse is never tolerated. Don't accept it, physical or verbal. Don't limit yourself. Be adventurous. Be true to your convictions. Be a doer, not a follower unless it is up the ladder of success. Remember to think and plan before you leap — impulsive actions without thinking can get you in trouble, but your instincts need to be listened to.

"By making good decisions early in the novel of life, your past won't come back to haunt you as you can look at yourself in the mirror later and say, well done.

"For those who are right behind me, in their 30s and 40s, do what you want to do with your life now and don't wait to invest in you further. Keep God and family in the forefront. You will find the strength you need. If family and friends are not there for you, God always is!"

## Mary Staples

"I was awaked to my aging when I attended a social function and noticed we all looked alike. We had the same look. I used to be the young one in the group.

"My greatest pleasure in getting older has been being able to be in a position to enjoy time and space for myself. I can now enjoy taking one day at a time and enjoying the moment. But what makes me most unhappy about this process is the weight I've gained.

"I think what bothers me most about the younger generation is babies having babies and having no interest in education. I'd like to see them strive to do more."

### Mary's Recipe:

"Young women should plan for their future and think positive. Exercising and being active is important as well as surrounding yourself with good books, good music and positive people."

## Karole Turner Campbell

"There has been no wake-up call indicating that I am in an older category of mature people. I say this because life, to me, is a series of wake-up calls that if gone unanswered, will lead to living, not death. I don't relate to age or aging characteristics.

When some so-called age-appropriate symptom pops up, I deal with it in one of two ways:

a) Acceptance (i.e., gray hair)

b) Modification and refocusing (i.e., coloring my hair)

"My greatest pleasure in maturing is to finally understand that I don't need to or have to please others. I know that sounds strange coming from such a self-assured Scorpion. But, hey, the reality is that our inner-selves are not always as secure as the outer picture we present.

"My greatest unhappiness is that I did not do this sooner!

"My concerns for teens are that they are rushing into physical maturity and gratification without the necessary spiritual and intellectual maturity, and that because of so many unplanned pregnancies, these young mothers/fathers do not have the strategies, knowledge, perspective or skills to responsibly nurture their children. Another concern is the level of literacy of young people. They can decode reading materials, but they often lack the ability to comprehend, analyze, synthesize or evaluate what they read, hear or see."

**Karole's Recipe:**

"My advice for the generation behind us/me:

a) Live. Living is growing; growing is learning; learning is acquiring and using knowledge. Stagnation is death.

b) Live purposefully. Everyday, seek ways to make your life and the people you touch better — better, richer and freer!"

# Kicking the Recipe Around the Table
## Wake Up and Smell the Coffee

1. What is your attitude about celebrating your next birthday?

2. Do you lie or avoid conversations about your age?

3. Is there an age you've repeated more than twice?

4. What was your best age?

5. Do you feel as sexually attractive as you felt ten years ago?

6. Do you feel out of place with 20- and 30-year-old women?

7. Would you feel comfortable dating a man fifteen years younger; ten years younger; five years younger; two years younger?

8. Explain your answer to number 7.

9. Is your state of mind, spirit and body better than ten years ago?

10. What experiences can you share with your family and community?

# Learn to Bake Your Own Cake

In 1983, Ben Badikiyan, former editor of The Washington Post, wrote in his book, "The Media Monopoly," that fifty corporations control newspapers, publishing, television and the movie industry. Only fourteen years later, the monopoly was in the hands of less than twenty corporations.

## The Image-Makers — Creating the Beauty Standard

America's image-makers did not have Asian, Black or even most white women in mind when they first created the beauty standards with which most people are familiar.

However, to placate the female consumers who don't fit the original mold, advertisers have attempted to include a wider racial group of women in the equation. The fact that ethnic women have to obliterate much of their original ethnic looks to approximate the look of white women is another matter.

Then, several years ago, a peculiar thing happened. White women started to avail themselves of the latest plastic-surgery innovations to take on many of the physical characteristics of Black women. The cosmetic industry exploded, largely ignited by white women who swelled thin lips with collagen and, by means of liposuction, padded their behinds with the displaced fat.

Tanning, the traditional means of approximating a Black look by white women, was exceeded by giving European features a boost by wedding them to an African aesthetic. Tellingly, as with the temporary nature of the appropriated white tan, this new look is not designed to be permanent.

Another effect of white women adopting a Black look is that the features take on a cache it never had on the original owners.

There are extremely destructive images of womanly beauty out there. They fall somewhere between the Barbie doll, a Bay Watch babe and a 19-year-old, size 2 runway model. Those extreme body shapes are not representative of women of any group.

Sadly, the marketing of these images has taken a toll on many females easily influenced by fashion trends. By chasing the illusion of beauty, many women — young and old — do irreparable physical harm to themselves. And what is illusion, after all?

According to Webster's dictionary, illusion is "a false idea, conception, belief or opinion, not in accord with the facts or an unreal, deceptive, misleading appearance or image, or a false perception, conception or interpretation of what one sees." An abnormal illusion goes by the name of hallucination.

## De-mystifying the White Woman as a Beauty Standard

Since bulimia/novas is predominant in the white female population, it's an indication that many white women feel they do not meet the standard of beauty most image-makers set. At the same time, white women's anxiety over having bodies they consider too thin is wide spread. Average-sized white women are not the standard, either.

In reality, no one human being is the standard. As with the epic beauty of Venus of lore, a singular physical ideal is only a myth. Tragically, too many white girls and women have died from starvation in search of an illusionary beauty. Reality says they are not the only females who fall victim to mythology.

The need in white culture to be thin at any cost has been too often a death knell. As I said, trying to live up to fiction is an unfair and unwholesome task. The negative consequences are often fatal.

On the other hand, Black women know that the media — with notable exceptions — do not project us, as a racial group, as being sexual or sensual, or having highly desirable feminine attributes. If African American women have a global image, it is clouded by the mixed messages sent by America's taboo-honored, startled embrace.

While all people are unique, it is safe to venture that it would be difficult to find a large number of African American women who are in counseling for bulimia/novas. Generally, it is not a Black cultural tendency to binge on food, then immediately vomit or purge the contents of the stomach by taking fast-acting laxatives to remain thin.

Many Black women are on the heavier end of the weight scale. With full tops and fuller bottoms, some Sisters put the "full" in full-bodied. In conversations over high-calorie meals, we laugh at anorexic runway models that would look pregnant if they swallowed a grape.

If American slavery served any purpose other than building this country on the whip-scarred backs of our ancestors, it was to set us free from illusions. Since white society had no beauty expectations of us, we created, along with jazz and blues, beauty standards of our own. Unfortunately, as with many enslaved people, Black folk adopted the same ideas of beauty as their enslavers.

With the exception of a nanosecond known as the 1960s, many Black peoples' deep-seated psychological unhappiness over dark skin and kinky hair hasn't changed much in four hundred years. While dreadlocks are flaunted alongside braids and the classic Coke of hair, the Afro, miracle blonde Black women of various generations are sprouting like so many Midwestern wheat fields.

Another curious choice is blonde dreadlocks. There's a confusing look that virtually screams bi-tress-ual. It's not a shoulder-length stretch to say that the Reverend Jesse Jackson's Rainbow Coalition has been reborn on the red, blonde, purple and orange heads of African American women. If we haven't overcome, we have over colored.

The value that image-makers and some Black men place on light skin and on long, straight hair keeps Black women determined to have long, straight hair and lighten up. For many Black females, hair "going back" is, sure enough, terror time.

## White Women Caught in the Hype

Slick marketing campaigns and, much about nature itself, cause men to desire large-breasted women. With less restraints on what's allowed to go out over the airwaves, situation comedies and talk shows regularly refer to melons, jugs and boobs.

Howard Stern, the king of all mediocrity, asks attention-starved women to bare their breasts. Between his radio show and his cable TV show, he's degraded more women than the Antebellum South. The main difference is, as opposed to sexually exploited Black females, the predominantly white female breast-bearers on the Stern show are willing participants in their own exploitation.

The models of beauty from Hollywood's past were movie stars such as Betty Grable, Marlene Deitrich and Cyd Charisse, among many others. Although their generation's breasts were ogled, a perhaps displaced fascination was transferred to their legs, even to the point of movie studios insuring those legs for millions of dollars.

It must be hard for Generation X to imagine, but there was a time when the mere mention of a woman's legs was considered risqué. Although from a fifty-foot movie screen, Jane Russell's breasts looked like they belonged on Mount Rushmore, there was never a mention of her endowments in any of her movies.

Some Seasoned Women will recall or have heard about pin-up girls from World War II who were photographed to project qualities such as perfect legs and good old-fashioned American sexuality to, as they say, remind the boys in service what they were fighting for.

New York City has its own institution that uses women's legs to carry on a grand tradition. Radio City Music Hall's Rockettes present the old-school leg bedazzlement.

Today's trend is to give full exposure to women's breasts. If

Spring Break and New Orleans' Mardi Gras are any indication, young women flashing their breasts has replaced saying hello. It seems more than a bit hypocritical to arrest men in the proverbial raincoat who flash women while the happy breast flashers get promoted in videos promising fresh young things who are just wild and having fun.

## Naturally Beautiful White Women — an Endangered Species

It may or may not be true that blondes have more fun. What's certain is that there's such a proliferation of blonde women today that a false news story, emanating from England, that a scientific study had determined that in a few hundred years the recessive nature of the gene that creates blonde hair would spell the end of the natural blonde created a sensation.

Later, the story was proven to be false when English scientists denied any such study of that nature was ever undertaken. With so many bottle blondes on television today, reality TV is a misnomer.

It might be interesting to speculate whether some of the stars of yesteryear would have equal success, today. For instance, would Farrah Fawcett, with breasts in proportion to her size, have made the same splash today as she did twenty five years ago with Pamela Anderson's breast implants?

And what about the reverse? Would Jennifer Lopez and Toni Braxton have been as popular in the '40s without the self-promoting gambit of undressing for award ceremonies? Let's see, Lucille Ball as a blonde? Naaaa! I love Lucy as a redhead.

There are consequences to plastic surgery, not all of them good. Some are even life altering. For example, in "Getting Over

Getting Older," by Letty Cottin Pogreb, there is a description of a woman's tortured experience after a face-lift. Pogreb writes: "In an article in Ms. magazine, she told how her corneas were bruised and her eyelids were stretched so tight that her eyes would not close and her eyeballs dried out, causing her excruciating pain. Though everything turned out fine, when she tallied the score, the negatives won out.

On the plus side: a smooth cheek and neck in. I have fewer lines. I know more truths about myself. On the minus side: serious eye problems. Fear of blindness. Hideous swelling and swollen eyes. Numb face and neck, which may last for months. A nasty fight with my husband. Loss of identity. Long-lasting scabbing. Loss of weeks of work. Lack of exercise for six weeks. The results last only four to eight years. After that, it sags and bags, again. Cost $5,300 (1986) plus eye-doctor bills." Page 133

In "Backlash," Susan Faludi writes: "For breast implants, in at least 20% of the cases, repeat surgery was required to remedy the ensuing pain, infection, blood clots or implant ruptures. A 1987 study in the annals of plastic surgery reported that the implants failed as much as 50 percent of the time and had to be removed.

In 1988, investigators at the FDA's Product Surveillance division found that the failure rate of breast implants was among the highest of any surgery-related procedure under their purview." Page 219

What if the waif look of Twiggy and Audrey Hepburn comes back? Would women with enhanced 38B and C breasts be seen bouncing around in movies and on TV? Perhaps not, but one thing is true. Plastic surgeons would enjoy return business by removing breast implants they originally inserted.

The March/April 2001 premiere issue of The AARP/MM magazine included an article entitled "Everything You Always Wanted to Know about Cosmetic Surgery but Were Afraid to Ask." It was an overview of cosmetic procedures Brenda Casale listed in the order of their popularity. Here are some of Casale's findings.

# Everything You Always Wanted to Know about Cosmetic Surgery but Were Afraid to Ask

## Non-Surgical Procedures

### Chemical Peel

*Cost: $743  Recovery Time: 1-2 Weeks*

A chemical peel solution (alpha hydroxyl acids or the harsher phenol is applied to the face to burn away the skin's top layers. New, healthier-looking skin emerges during the healing process. ***Risks & Relations:*** Complications are rare, but include infection, scarring and flare up of skin conditions (allergies, cold sores). Permanent skin color changes can occur. Phenol peels eliminate skin's ability to tan.

### Botox Injection

*Cost: $432  Recovery Time: No down time*

Botulinum (a nerve toxin) is injected into the muscle near facial wrinkles. It blocks nerve impulses and temporarily paralyzes the muscles that cause wrinkles, smoothing them out. The effects last an average of four months. ***Risks & Relations:*** Risks include an allergic reaction to the toxin, swelling, redness, bruising, numbness and headaches. Rarely, a reduced blinking reflex, which may last for several months, can cause corneal exposure and ulceration.

## Laser Hair Removal
### Cost: $492  Recovery Time: No down time
A laser targets the hair follicle, destroying it and preventing hair re-growth. **Risks & Relations:** Any redness or blistering should disappear within a day. Skin discoloration may occur, but it is usually temporary. There is a rare risk of permanent scarring.

## Collagen Injection
### Cost: $354  Recovery Time: No down time
Collagen (a natural protein) is injected to plum up facial lines or add fullness to lips and backs of hands. Effects last a few months to a year. **Risks & Relations:** The main risk is an allergic reaction to the bovine collagen, which could cause swelling, redness or flu-like symptoms. There is rare risk of infection. Contour irregularities may occur.

## Laser Skin Resurfacing
### Cost: $2,383  Recovery Time: 1-2 Weeks
Layers of skin are removed with laser beam and as the healing process progresses, a new, healthier-looking skin emerges. The effects are long lasting. **Risks & Relations:** Infection and scarring are infrequent. There may be a flare-up of skin conditions (allergies, cold sores). Skin color changes or blotchiness may sometimes occur.

## Dermabrasion
### Cost: $1,383  Recovery Time: 7-10 Days
The skin is numbed and a small, rapidly spinning wheel with a surface similar to fine sandpaper removes the top layers of skin. New, healthier-looking skin emerges during the healing process.

*Risks & Relations:* Infection and abnormal healing are infrequent. Very rarely, people may develop raised or thickened scars, which are sometimes permanent. Permanent skin color changes can occur and the person may lose the ability to tan.

# Surgical Procedures

## Liposuction
*Cost: $2,322  Recovery Time: 1-2 Weeks*

Unwanted fat is vacuumed away by inserting a small hollow tube through tiny incisions in the skin. The tube is connected by a hose to a suctioning device. *Risks & Relations:* Risks include bleeding, infection and reactions to the anesthesia. Lack of sensation and skin discoloration may occur. The skin may appear rippled or baggy. Rarely, fat clots or blood clots could migrate to the lungs and cause death.

## Breast Augmentation
*Cost: $3,142  Recovery Time: 1-2 Weeks*

An incision is made through which an implant is inserted into a pocket either directly behind the breast tissue or underneath the pectoral muscle. The implant is then filled with saline. *Risks & Relations:* Risks include hematoma, infection and reactions to anesthesia. Changes in nipple or breast sensation are usually temporary. Scar tissue may harden around the implant. Breast implants may leak or break, requiring additional surgery.

## Breast Reduction
### Cost: $5,024  Recovery Time: 1-2 Weeks
Generally, three incisions are made. Excess breast tissue, fat and skin are removed and the nipple and areola are positioned higher. In men, a small incision is made near the edge of the areola. Excess fat is liposuctioned or cut out. *Risks & Relations:* Risks include bleeding, infection, reactions to anesthesia. May cause temporary (sometimes permanent) loss of sensation in the nipples or breasts. Scars are extensive and permanent.

## Face-Lift
### Cost: $5,135  Recovery Time: Within 2 weeks
Incisions are placed at the temples and in front of and behind the ear. The skin is lifted off the underlying tissue, excess fat is removed and underlying muscles are tightened. The skin is pulled back and the excess is removed. *Risks & Relations:* Complications include hematoma, infection, reactions to anesthesia and injury to the nerves that control facial muscles (usually temporary). Poor healing may result in excessive scarring.

## Tummy Tuck
### Cost: $4,215  Recovery Time: 1-3 Weeks
An incision is made across the lower abdomen. The skin is separated from the abdominal wall; the underlying muscle and tissue are brought together and tightened. The skin is then brought down and the excess is removed. *Risks & Relations:* Risks include bleeding, infection and reactions to anesthesia. Fluid may accumulate under the skin. Blood clots may develop, which could travel to the lungs. Decreases blood flow to the abdomen could cause skin loss, requiring a graft.

## Hair Transplant

*Cost: $3,184  Recovery Time: 2-5 days*

Small grafts of hair-bearing skin are removed from the back and sides of the scalp and transplanted to bald areas. ***Risks & Relations:*** Risks include bleeding, infection, scarring, an unnatural look and the failure of the grafts to "take."

# Black Women Caught in the Hype

The fact that cosmetic surgery is more affordable now makes it more available to average Black women. So far, Black celebrities and upwardly mobile, professional women are mainly the ones getting plastic surgery. Most other Black women have either not been able to afford it or have chosen not to have any procedures done.

However, if Black women were completely happy with themselves, the Korean-dominated hair-care industry would crash. Korean shopkeepers sell the long, straight hair so many of us purchase because so few of us were born with it.

Movable hair, that Black female fantasy, swinging off our shoulders like a white woman's hair, either in individual foot-long braids or straight, loose falls is the closest thing to being the product of a bi-racial marriage — or a descendant of Thomas Jefferson — to getting what oppressed people used to call "good" hair.

Madam C.J. Walker's invention of the hot comb made her millions, getting the naps out of our hair. Today, in addition to the handy hot comb, chemicals straighten Black hair. After the hair damage is done, Korean beauty supply shops provide the quick fixes to cover the bald spots.

For many Black women, hair they're happy with continues to be illusive. White women have their own unhappy issues with their hair. They call it a bad hair day. However, if there were any seniority rights for hair phraseology, we would win out based on our coinage of terms concerning centuries of white brainwashing, terms such as bad hair and good hair.

One thing is certain. Feelings about what constitutes bad hair and good hair have lasted longer than a day. Without wanting to admit it, as a Black person, you know — instinctively — that those feelings are carried by your mother and your father, as it was by their mother and father and theirs, all the way back to the African start to an American destination You know, instinctively, that it pervades the recesses of the mind of the Blackest militant that ever cursed his white brethren.

Skin-bleaching products, to take the black away from the faces of some Black women, have always been popular. Many Blacks in show business, male and female, seem to get lighter faces the more successful they become. Using that equation, Michael Jackson is by far the most successful former Black person in show business. From the days of "I'm Black and I'm proud," we've come a long way, baby.

For those of us who are afraid to chance the side effects of chemical peels and other drastic, ghostly changes, we can always fall back on traditional favorites such as Nadinola and Noxzema for a paler appearance. The rest of the body can remain dark, as long as the face is as light as possible. It's as though no one notices dark backs, arms and legs.

Although a relatively small number of Black women have cosmetic surgery, they aren't free of a need to control their image. Within the last fifteen years, the professional manicure and pedicure have become popular. Nail shops have sprung up in many urban neighborhoods and malls.

Asian women have developed a nail salon industry by providing a service that was usually reserved for the more affluent. Today, local access has taken the business of nails to another level. The nails of many women and teen girls resemble long, detailed art objects. Out of necessity, many women have mastered the art of functioning with dysfunctional fingernails.

Not surprisingly, these female talons interfere with routines like: cleaning the vaginal area, handling tampons and sanitary napkins, closing zippers and snaps on clothing, brushing teeth, healthy food preparation and effectively using a computer.

Women, seeking glamour, compromise their health by ignoring the need for good hygiene, all for the sake of beautiful hands. Things like spreading germs and the permanent damage done to the natural nail is ignored.

Glamour is a new luxury for many women of color. They are actively courted by a beauty industry slow to learn that they could grow their business by adopting a strategy of inclusion. Services such as facials, body massages and electrolysis are new to working-class women. Traditionally, hairdressers in neighborhood beauty shops or in a neighbor's kitchen were the providers of most beauty treatment.

Women of color should remember the neighborhood Black women who are 85-plus-years old. We think of some history as long past, but we still have women who are the direct descendants of grand parents that were born during slavery.

Black freedom is less than a hundred and fifty years old, in a country that claims to be a little over three hundred years old. Black women's true beauty hasn't had time to internalize. The clockwork for the Black-beauty pendulum swings back and forth, from slavery to the present.

Our self-esteem is still culturally tied to the conflicts between the house slaves and field slaves. This animosity between Blacks was based on the preferential treatment and status conferred on American house slaves who were chosen for less grueling labor because their features closer resembled their masters, by reasons of tribal origins or centuries of mixing blood with them. Things like light skin and fine hair were carried to modern-day Black culture as a serious divide among us.

Issues such as weight, breast size and face-lifts are not high on our priority list. Although white America, in its understandable shame, would like to pretend slavery was as in a fairy tale, long ago and far away, it is still too close for many of us to be concerned about cosmetic surgery, particularly at this time in our Black Seasoned Womanhood.

We need time to evolve from being excited by owning things we can't afford. But, give us another twenty years when the generation of aging hip-hoppers (perhaps our first generation of Black spoiled brats, if you don't count Baby Boomers) develop standards to elevate the character of their children, accept social responsibility for their communities and learn that their value is not determined by clothing designer price tags. Then we'll see positive change. I may be optimistic, but the hip-hop generation is better equipped to set standards for themselves than we were at their age.

Technology has overexposed them to everything imaginable on a global level and given them a sense of a techno-community. They feel connected in some Web beat of understanding around the world that is their drum. Their view of the world and how they fit in it isn't the same as ours. The future mindset of the Black and Latina people is in the hands of our current generation. Of the future, only one thing is certain: a different and new marketing hype will be devised to snare them, too.

## Blacks Not Taken Seriously as a Market

In the 1930s, some sixty-five years after slavery, the National Negro Business League conducted a study to determine the living habits and income ($1.65 billion) of Black consumers. Montgomery Ward, Lever Brothers and Anheuser-Busch were some of the companies that sponsored the study. Page 424(5).

A second investigation into how Black dollars were spent didn't take place for another fifty years when, in November 1983, a Black-owned firm targeted the minority market for serious consideration and fact-finding.

It was then that Burrell Advertising was hired by Proctor & Gamble to develop marketing for Crest Toothpaste that was culturally sensitive to Blacks. Page 440.

Although great strides were made during the early '80s, the surge did not continue. The Black-owned advertising firms made up of Burrell Advertising, Mingo-Jones, Uniworld, Lockhart & Pettus, J.P. Martin & Associates and Proctor & Gardner collectively made $155 million in 1985. Although a substantial sum in an area not known for Black representation, when compared with the profits of mainstream agencies, it was a dismally small share of the market. Page 442 (44).

As a group, Black women are greater buyers of clothes than they are concerned with physical renovation. I remember in the late '70s when Black women purchased trendy, French-cut jeans and struggled to squeeze their naturally round butts into a space intended for the flatter backsides of white women. If ever we needed reminding, designers let us know they weren't designing clothes for non-European types.

There were some slapstick moments involving French-cut jeans that were worthy of a silent film comedy. These impossible-to-get-into jeans caused a woman I know to lay on the bed, the floor or anyplace firm to squeeze into the low-cut, tapered waist and pencil thin pant legs. It took both of us to get them on her. I held the zipper and waistband while she pushed her stomach flat and sucked in her waistline.

My contortionist friend held her shoulders high to stretch herself as far out and become thinner by holding her breath for as long as possible. Inch by resisting inch, I tugged the beleaguered zipper up to the closure snap. The snap gave up and closed. One sneeze from my constricted friend would've freed more Black flesh than Abraham Lincoln.

Before Terry MacMillan ever thought of waiting to, my friend exhaled and she miraculously remained inside her French-cut bondage. It may only be a rumor, but I heard that her zipper's now in the Smithsonian.

The silent film continued when girlfriend and I got to the party. She wanted to sit at the table and eat, but she couldn't bend her knees to lower herself in the seat. I looked around to see she was not alone. There was a roomful of Black women in French-cut jeans, standing because they had no choice.

They leaned and profiled, but few were able to sit and if they did, they didn't stay for more than fifteen minutes. It was amazing! My girlfriend's feet were swollen because of a lack of circulation and her throat was dry because she couldn't drink anything. She knew that she couldn't unzip her jeans and use the ladies' room; she'd never get back in them.

Some of us may have amnesia now, but believe me, back in the day, Black women put themselves through the tortures of the damned to jump aboard a fashion train that came from the north — the North Pole, that is.

## Naturally Beautiful Black Women

Most mature Black women are not convinced that they need to take out a $10,000 loan to have the skin pulled back tight on their faces. It's not about the face or the basketball boobs, anyway. As a woman walks by, follow a man's eyes. Nine times out of ten, a man's eyes are riveted on a woman's backfield in motion.

Full breasts are nice, but the power of the booty could make a bishop kick out a stain-glass window. And what's more, we women know a shapely ass has been a man magnet since before we learned to walk upright or walk in those proverbial pump-me-hard high heels.

It is said of Helen of Troy, hers was the face that launched a thousand ships. Maybe history didn't report the real part of her anatomy that drove men to war.

## Black and White Women Can Overcome the Hype

Black Seasoned Women's resistance to plastic surgery may inspire other groups of women to bypass the self-altering procedures. Seasoned Black and white women can fight the illogical appeal of the cosmetic and fashion industries' marketing campaigns.

We were battle-hardened during the civil rights movement. That southern primer in grassroots protest gave us skills to not only resist the status quo, but to change one that works against our best interests.

Black women make temporary changes to their appearance, such as with wigs, weaves and fake nails. But most are not willing to alter their appearance with plastic surgery.

Maybe our slave history and instincts for survival have helped us to know where to draw the line. Being Black and female has made us immune to many adverse images. Aunt Jemima, fat maids and mammies have demeaned us since before the invention of television and film. As a result, we've developed thick skins to protect us from being psychologically crushed.

At least, a number of us have. It is to the many who haven't developed a protective, hard veneer that I especially extend the spirit of the Seasoned Woman.

Fortunately for the Seasoned Woman of color, many seasoned men appreciate women with flesh on their bones. Although the reality is that men and women of all races are mixing with more freedom than ever before (a fact that TV and the movies exaggerates for maximum profit), most people still choose to be with lovers who look much like themselves. I salute Black and Latino men who cherish our shared African roots and the large, shapely female asses that Mother Africa sculpted on us almost as a refrain to God's "In the Beginning…"

Spiritual identification of the body as a living temple is sacrosanct for many Black women. Tampering with the body for cosmetic reasons is a spiritual transgression for some of them. Across different cultures, the face of what an attractive aging woman looks like varies, greatly. An informal observation of southern white men informs me that they frequently marry women who might be classified as full-figured.

As Seasoned Black and white women, we must open the lines of communication to help each other on issues detrimental to all women. White female executives, as they escape the corporate glass ceiling, can change the way women of color are seen.

It may be a lot to ask of women, in a challenging arena, determined to prove they belong. And, certainly, the corporate world has rarely been known for altruistic innovation. However, the larger question is, why assume a position of power if that power can't be used? If power newly gained is not used, we have another kind of ceiling restraining women, not glass maybe, but a barrier to female equality.

As Supreme Court Justice, Clarence Thomas, proves with every high-court vote, people don't always side with those with whom they share similar cultural attributes. Unfortunately, that list of turncoats is a long one and won't be given space here.

In spite of all the black sheep in white wolves' clothing, I am still convinced that white women are our best chance to change the many negative images of women of color that have been promoted by their white husbands, fathers, brothers and, sometimes, themselves.

Some white women producers are equally guilty of not including attractive Black women and Seasoned Women in entertainment venues. I don't know if the HBO series "Sex in the City" is produced by a woman, but it is an example of the type of exclusion only seen this side of a Woody Allen movie.

According to these chroniclers of city life, there're only white people in New York City, with an occasional UFO sighting of a Black person. Maybe these types of depictions of the city should be called "desired-reality TV."

The white male pervades prime time television, as news anchors, talk show hosts and sports announcers. While cable stations try to reverse the skewed color scheme of network TV by presenting Black, Latin and Asian on-camera talent, the network's big three (ABC, NBC and CBS), most noticeably on the local news level, pair a woman of color with a white male anchor.

As Seasoned Black and white women, we recognize the dangers in skewed images of America's reality. One result is that a society that is culturally insensitive and ignorant is allowed to go on living with a warped sense of non-white peoples' capabilities and worth. The consequences are potentially hurtful to all aging women.

Instead of sitting back and resting on our substantial laurels, what can mature women do to protest the absence of all but the young? We can write letters, fax, e-mail and call companies who consistently exclude mature womanhood.

We need to make it known when the rare portrayal of an older person is insulting and used for the sake of cheap laughs. With the proliferation of computers to register our objections, there is no excuse not to weigh in with our unified voice of indignation.

The revolution in the '60s and '70s may not have instilled changes that all have lasted, but some significant ones remain. Compared to that struggle, this new struggle for the recognition of Seasoned Women is a piece of cake, with the registration of protest only a computer or phone call away.

We have no excuse, except apathy, to hold us back. We have larger numbers, our money and, when widowed, the money of our late husbands. However, we must remember that it's only power, if we use it. Let network sponsors and producers know how we feel.

## Become Pro-Active

As Seasoned Women, we must mentor younger women to avoid the insanity of starvation and body sculpting as the answer to beauty in America. We must advocate more openly for the fullness of our bodies and our natural complexions.

Before white women entered the job market in significant numbers, society had a healthy image reflected by the likes of Marilyn Monroe who, by today's standards, would be considered closer to a bovine than the model of a beautiful body.

Never mind that there was little healthy about Monroe's mental state. I am referring to what she represented for the society of her time as compared to influential women of the times in which we live.

What is the alternative for white men, if white women defy trendy, skinny images and embrace their natural curves? Would they desert them? That's doubtful. Seasoned white men will do what they've always done: love their Seasoned Women.

It is important to remember that many fashion houses and marketing agencies are run by men who have no sexual interest in women. Homosexual men who view women as merely business interests aren't the drum majors for maximum female health.

While the desire for a profitable bottom line is the goal of any businessman, straight or gay, it's undeniable that homosexual and heterosexual men view women differently. It's that difference that influences what images of women get promoted and, if part of a successful campaign, get assumed by women seeking always to be on top of fashion.

# Reshaping the Image-Makers

The passage of time has proven to us that society has the potential to modify and even reverse its value system, through advertising and public awareness campaigns, to re-direct behavior.

As a society, we have witnessed public opinion's influence on behavioral changes, when powerful marketing strategies are applied in the right places.

Media assisted in eliminating the allure of cigarette smoking, promoting physical fitness, cholesterol control, buckling seat belts and wearing helmets for biking and skating. The positive influences of the public service announcements and promo spots featuring celebrities grew over a period of time. The result was that life-threatening behaviors of the past changed forever.

Seasoned Woman is the name I propose be used to describe women of a certain age into the new millennium and beyond. My hope is that it replaces the imagery that comes to mind of a Senior Citizen. The term doesn't conjure a picture of a mood-swinging, menopausal freak or a dried-up, matronly has-been.

As we know, language pushes the senses. The term Seasoned Woman infers something extraordinary, something of which a skinny, twenty-something woman has no concept.

The Seasoned Woman separates herself from the sea of immature girl-images of the 20th Century that were used as touchstones for media purposes. The Seasoned Woman is a title that we have boldly earned and can use with a wicked smile.

We don't need or want to feel less than women, as we feel when we continue to use negative terms to identify ourselves. Use this mantra to stop referring to yourself in terms that are not complimentary. Names should invoke the best feelings within you and other people. I know in my heart that I am a Seasoned Woman and, more than likely, you are also.

In the Modern Maturity, MM, magazine 2001 March/April issue, in a piece called "Eyes Wide Shut," Mary P. Willis shared her feelings about having completed cosmetic surgery. In part, she says, "We all know that we live in a culture that idolizes youth and disdains aging. But for someone who thought she had a strong sense of self, who considers herself a feminist and comes from a long line of beautiful and intelligent women, I realize to my dismay, that I was no more comfortable in my own skin than the average consumer.

And like many women, I'd come to believe the stereotype — which is, better to be young and wrinkle-free than a woman who looks her age....

If my cosmetic surgery taught me anything, it was that whether I like it or not, I'm going to get old; just like everybody else. And rather than fight it, I might as well embrace it.

There's a great line, in Sunset Boulevard, a film I saw on television right after my surgery. 'There's nothing tragic about being 50,' William Holden says to Gloria Swanson, as he's walking out on her. 'Not unless you try to be 25.'"

# Kicking the Recipe Across the Table
## Learning to Bake Your Own Cake

1. Do you feel others see your true character? Explain.

2. What is your level of satisfaction with your self-image on a scale from one, the lowest, to ten, the highest?

3. If you had a miracle wish that would come true to change your mental or physical state, which would you select?

4. In a few words, what sums up your total package?

5. In your opinion, what are your best assets? Your shortcomings?

6. What is the hardest personal obstacle you've had to overcome without the assistance of anyone except yourself?

7. Do you celebrate your achievements more than you complain about the hard times?

8. Who do you blame for your rough times?

9. Are you in the parade or watching it go by without you?

# Get Off Your Ass and Get a Life

Verna left college to become the major caregiver/mother for her deceased sister's three children. Vera witnessed the slow decay of Sue Ellen's family, as Sue Ellen cared for her husband for years until he died of complications caused by AIDS. Pneumonia ended Sue Ellen's life shortly thereafter.

Verna was left with Spencer, a three year old, Ashton six and Heather, fourteen, to raise. Verna's decision to take on the role of head of household for her nieces and nephews saved them from being separated in the foster care system of California. With very little financial assistance from the state and a lot of long hours of work from Verna, the family remained together.

Unfortunately, within a year, Heather gave birth to a son. Verna became a 22-year-old grandmother. Heather dropped out of school and continued a relationship with the baby's unemployed father.

Three years later, Verna took on the responsibility of raising the baby, Craig, after his mother moved out. Spencer and Ashton continued school, but had no serious interest in attending college.

However, Verna's role as mother and grandmother for her grandnephew paid dividends. Craig was an honor student and received a partial scholarship to a state university in Southern California.

Now 39 years old, Verna was struggling to get Craig through college. Craig's mother and the two oldest nephews were incapable of living on their own as responsible adults. They were in and out of the house, and between jobs and/or relationships. They contributed no support to the household.

Looking down the short road to the big 5-0 was terrifying for Verna. During one of my follow-up sessions, at a staff-development series sponsored by her agency, she spoke of aging as a curse. Her honest expressions of bitterness, anger and hopelessness to her discussion group participants burned deeply into my heart.

Verna came to the seminar on her off day. She stayed late to attend a repeat of my anti-violence, anti-verbal abuse workshop for the night staff. The following day, Verna became my shadow.

Our mutual attraction was cemented in our shared work in community HIV/AIDS education and prevention. She was the program co-coordinator/counselor for her agency. In fact, her life was consumed with fighting the disease that killed her sister and devastated her family. The workshop sessions had removed the band-aid from her open wound.

At some point, we talked about ourselves as women and not professionals, while eating a box lunch on the campus grounds of the college. Cautiously, like a young girl talking to her mother about a first kiss, Verna confessed her secret desires. As her dreams spilled out, I felt privileged that she allowed me into her private world.

She told me that she wanted to get married and finish college. She said she wanted to have a baby of her own, before it was too late. She wanted a pretty house to decorate, without considering anyone except herself. And most of all, she wanted to cash a check, hold the money in her hand and spend it on whatever she wanted for herself for a change

Although her dreams were within reason, she felt too old and out-of-step with the new, high-tech world to try. Instead of stepping into the shoes that would have to be filled to accomplish her goals, Verna indulged herself in overeating. She lived to go to new places to eat with her equally miserable girlfriends. They ate themselves into immobility.

Verna surrounded herself with girlfriends that she could depend on to give her a sympathetic ear. Together, they could bemoan their disappointments without moving forward. They lived in a comfort zone called social paralysis.

Verna is like many mid-life women that give up on themselves because they feel overwhelmed. I call it social paralysis. Social paralysis is when you're miserable where you are, but feel absolutely unable to change the negative condition that is paralyzing you.

The recipe to satisfy Verna's needs is the hardest one of all. I call it, "Get Off Your Ass and Get a Life."

## Getting Started

Verna's teen years were spent being a caregiver to a dying sister and the remainder was spent being breadwinner, mother and grandmother. Before menopause ended Verna's chances at childbirth and lessened her chances for marriage, she had to quickly get herself moving.

Verna was going to have to buy into a serious life change, one that called for behaviors that would satisfy her desires for happiness.

I remember when I was very young and had to face my fear of the unknown, without the benefit of a Seasoned Mentor. Then, I realized the value of life lessons from recipes. Many recipes were passed on to me from the women in my life. I began relying on them as a formula for myself.

Sharing my personal experience with Verna was a chance to end her perception of my being some kind of super woman. Verna saw me as someone incapable of identifying with her feelings of being overwhelmed and vulnerable.

We Seasoned Women must be receptive and humble, to allow our human side to show. Our exposed flaws can be something that encourages younger, insecure women to seek us out for the help they desperately need.

## Getting Started, Again

This recipe is generic for any economic, sex, gender, age or racial grouping. The end product will result in a changed life. Although it is difficult and time consuming, I use this formula a lot. It helps shape my image of an accomplished, successful Seasoned Woman. I'm sure it will help you, too.

## Essential Ingredients:

Courage and more courage

Clean sheets of paper

Pen/pencil

A beautifully bound book

A large box of soft tissues

And an abundance of faith

### Instructions:

Start

Begin by laying out a sheet of paper on a flat surface like a kitchen table or desk. Don't use a computer. A computer is too detached from your body pulse to connect you personally to your feelings.

Using a pen or pencil, write down everything and everyone you blame for making your present situation unacceptable.

Place what you recognize and understand to be the biggest culprit on a second sheet of paper.

Copy the culprit onto several index cards and tape them to the refrigerator, medicine cabinet, closet doors, etc.

Save the original full sheet of paper in a safe place for future reference.

Live with it in your conscious mind. Read the culprit out loud every time you see it on the index card, as you go about your life.

If you think you discovered the culprit and the pain of your existence, and it doesn't push any buttons in your belly or brain every time you see it, you may be blaming the wrong issue for your condition. Go back to the original sheet of paper and select another culprit.

Repeat the process until the original list is exhausted.

Finally, when you get to the real culprit, you'll feel a rush of agitation. It will be a strong negative reaction. You may be surprised that what you thought was the culprit is not the problem, but the symptom.

Because the symptom is more apparent than the cause of the pain, you shouldn't mistake one for the other. For example, if you notice a tremendous weight gain in the spring, you attribute the fat to the  quart of double fudge ice cream you ate at bedtime all winter. It is important to recognize that the ice cream isn't the culprit. It's only the symptom. The culprit is the pain that drove you to eat the ice cream, night after night.

When you seriously sift through your blame sheet, you will discover that you are the culprit, if there is one. When the last suspect proves to be you, it's time to put all of the symptoms in the trash. You have been hiding behind them long enough.

So, get off your ass! Move on with the hard stuff in your life.

The signs of discontent will be made more obvious and be prioritized. Now that you got over blaming other people, places and things for your situation in life, you feel more in charge. Satisfaction isn't immediate, but you're more in control of what pushes your buttons.

Depending on the length of the blame list, this process may take months to complete. The need to lay blame on something or someone to be responsible for your condition is time wasted.

It can never lead to a positive result because it gives power over your happiness to an outside force.

After the emotions about your current situation calm down, you are ready to go forward. You can begin to cook in your pot and prepare your meal.

Next, separate the yolk from the egg white. The white of the egg (the support for life fluid) is to be symbolically placed in the lovely bound Life-Planning book you purchased. The egg white goes in first. It's the core of your truth. The transparent nature of truth and its consistency will assist in holding together many of the ingredients that will come later. The body of nutrition will support the internal work to be done.

When you begin the renovation of "self," always have dependable sustenance. Change creates stress and apprehension because of the nature of the unknown. Therefore, it is crucial to surround your yolk (your core) with all the sturdy "good stuff" that makes you feel worthy and valuable.

## Organize Your Life Plan

On the first page of your life-planning book, place your name in the center. On the following pages, jot down all of your best qualities, the people in your life who are there for you unconditionally, obstacles you've overcome and the best experience of your life. Leave the additional pages to be filled with good feelings as you remember them, in the days to come.

Positive accomplishments will be recorded first, to remind you of your strengths. It is a quick overview of what is good and wonderful about your life. Feeling good about yourself increases your level of confidence that you'll need to rely on when the going gets rough.

The second half of the book is the results of goals you set out to achieve. This is your yolk. It will take longer to fill because this is where preparation for the small dishes will yield to presentation of the whole gourmet meal.

Now, it's time to use your main ingredient — courage. You must be brave to work through the change process. The process of disciplined "self work" to rid you of social paralysis will force you to become pro-active.

Being focused on working on your self, with your mental health at stake, will yield successful results if you answer the following exercise questions:

*1. Where are you, now?*
*2. Where do you want to be?*
*3. What steps are you willing to take to get there?*
*4. When do you plan to get there?*

The Vernas of the world will need many tissues for question numbers 1 and 2. These questions open the gate to facing up to current realities. The honest answers to them force people to stop: feeling sorry for themselves, stop blaming circumstances of race, economics, sex, education or even the destructive power of the devil.

Many people who find themselves constantly unhappy about their lives are usually procrastinating dreamers. They are not especially lazy, but their sense of responsibility is weighted in favor of other people's needs instead of a healthy balance that includes them.

Verna typifies the martyr. She sacrificed her youth, which should have been filled with self-discovery and adventures, to become a surrogate mother.

During the childbearing years when Verna was young, she put all of her time into being an overworked mother and grandmother for her late sister's children. Now, there was little to show for almost a half century of living. Verna felt cheated.

We have all been down a similar street. Feeling unfulfilled and hopeless is not a status reserved for poor, uneducated females. Many 50-year-old high-income women and men know the feeling.

Facing your own demons takes courage. The box of tissues I mentioned at the beginning of the Life Plan will be well used to dry the tears for lost years and relationships.

## The Stove is Ready

President Truman, a fellow Missourian, had an expression: "If you can't take the heat, stay out of the kitchen."

The second section of your life-planning book is traumatic. That's why it's important to write down your feel-good notations in the first section. No pain, no gain refers to your mental as well as your physical health.

Change is the desired outcome for this recipe. A reconstructed life is the goal. A baking dish filled with fresh peaches and spices spread between two layers of crust will not yield a pineapple upside down cake. The ingredients to a recipe yields a particular product. This recipe is for behavioral change.

For Verna to handle the heat, she had to develop a new language in referring to herself. Otherwise, she would remain in the same place.

Verna's ability to bear full responsibility for her situation and the consequences of change hinged on how well she was able to tap into her core.

The intrapersonal (internal) communication process provides access to information buried under years of clutter in the conscious and unconscious spirit.

Since Verna's overwhelmed state of mind didn't happen overnight, it took considerable time for her to break through. To become selfish without feeling guilty, she had to develop a new internal conversation.

Setting aside communication solitary time, to review your issues, isn't a common preoccupation. Usually "self" gets pushed back to make room for other situations and you never get back to it.

Tuning into and listening to yourself keeps you in harmony with your spiritual core. That's where your personal God-mind centers your being. You must train yourself to listen and converse.

Otherwise, you go with the flow and react to life as opposed to being the creator of what happens to you. Verna was a chronic facilitator, to feeding whatever others hungered for in her family.

For constructive interpersonal communication, jot down a topic that only relates to you. Next, spend fifteen minutes listening and not speaking. What do you hear and feel? What is the purpose of your life?

This will take time and many conversations. Answers will begin to come in your sleep, while walking down the street or while eating. If you take control of your life, the internal will speak to you.

Once you master the technique, you can take deliberate actions that propel your life. With unusual courage, you gain a new freedom. However, beware of resistance. Your family and friends may not accept your new focus on your needs. They may discourage and resent your changed behavior.

For millions of women like Verna to achieve number 3, they will need the same amount of determination they showed in serving the needs of others. To know what steps to take and take them is a big order for those who have lived with buried dreams.

Number 4 creates the motion of progression. Timelines are important. To have a sense of moving forward, it is essential to know the order of your expectations. Closures can then be followed by expectations of what's to come next.

Assigning a specific time frame to achieve a goal helps you to monitor the success of your mini-objectives. The process seems to move faster when deadlines are imposed and met.

Verna's looming deadline concerned having a child. The end of her childbearing period was near. If she was going to have a child, she couldn't hesitate. Getting pregnant might not happen to her in the traditional way, but it was something she could control. Few men appealed to Verna's high standards, so she had few dates. She was attracted to religious men — men who were tall, muscular, and who wanted marriage and children. She wanted a combination of The Rock and a preacher. Most of the men who fell into that rare category didn't show much interest in Verna. If she did go out with a high-profile man, it rarely went beyond the initial date.

Verna wanted a Prince Charming to rescue her from her misery. She wanted her children to have a good chance for success. Marrying "well" was her dream. The additional role of grandmother added to Verna's stress.

It was Verna's turn, but she felt too old and out of step to begin, again. Because I was an older woman, I became her mentor to pull her along the road to change.

Verna was ready for some concrete steps that would lead to a committed relationship and, eventually, a baby. With her inner hunger, a fulfilling life was more than possible.

Somewhere in her 50s, a woman discovers the difference between a side dish, an appetizer and a full meal. For most women, their 40s are the sorting years. By then, you have resolved the conflicting forces pulling at you and made peace with your demons.

I'm blessed to still have my mother just a phone call away. It saves me from making a lot of mistakes. I have learned to understand what she says to me out of love. I trust her when she says, "I know." After years preparing what I thought was the gourmet meal, I've discovered how much there always is to learn about cooking your own stew.

The success of the plan lies in the first step you take toward change. It sets the foundation for everything else to rest on.

Verna knew she needed something concrete to do that did not require a partner. After much research and consulting with me, Verna chose an activity where, at age 39, she could develop an interesting lifestyle.

Verna decided to become an amateur golfer. Her giant step into the unknown started with the purchase of a set of golf clubs from a Salvation Army store. The second step was to take golf lessons at the local community college. Her most expensive investment was finding discount travel rates for her two-week vacation. Golf would also allow her to meet men.

The instructor of Verna's golf theory class gave her several names of friends who were affiliated with the golf circuit. The contacts were welcomed in the event she wanted to get discounts to some of their member golf courses.

With a lot of hard work, Verna became a skilled amateur golfer. She read everything about golf she could find and she lost weight as a by-product of the sport.

Verna didn't have time to eat constantly or spend time with her girlfriends. Her social circle became more diverse.

Verna knew her limitations and capitalized on her strengths. As program coordinator, she volunteered to spearhead national projects to represent her local agency. The projects required her to maintain contact with key people on the national level. When the projects ended, Verna kept in contact with the network of people.

During Verna's work for her agency, she contributed fresh ideas and worked out a flexible schedule to cover evening and weekend groups. She needed her days free to shore up future career possibilities. Consequently, Verna stopped following the schedule that kept her in a box.

Verna organized a successful walk-a-thon for her HIV/AIDS organization. This put her in touch with many corporate sponsors who also did underwriting for golf tournaments.

Researching the sponsors of national golf tournaments, Verna located a Hawaiian golf clinic/retreat for amateurs. She used her contacts to attend at a discounted rate. As a reward for her volunteer work with the walk-a-thon, her agency gave her a bonus.

Verna's two-week Hawaiian vacation passed so quickly, she barely had enough time to wear all of her golf outfits. She discovered the meaning of casual golf attire the hard way. Her overstuffed bags remained packed with clothes she never got to wear. Her expensive room with the ocean view was only used for sleeping, showering and changing clothes.

Next time, Verna would be wiser. Had she been a more experienced traveler and golfer, she would have saved money and time spent shopping. Nevertheless, she returned from Hawaii inspired.

# Making Your World Change with You

Although Verna's children and grandchildren saw her actively pursuing a new hobby, for them the family dynamics were unchanged. Her brood eagerly awaited her return from Hawaii and a return to life, as they knew it.

Verna was changed. No longer could she be the unconsidered caregiver of old. The Hawaiian golf clinic was like a graduation for her. The entire vacation made her aware of what was possible.

Verna needed support to create a workable plan for her complete emancipation. She called upon a few of her favorite resource people who were recorded in the first section of her life-planning book.

Many of Verna's relationships with older women had ended because of her inability to lift herself out of the mire of martyrdom. However, Verna didn't want to be a super woman, anymore. It was unhealthy for her and counter-productive for the family.

Verna's makeover was at the point of no return, the place where most plans for change fail. They get put on the back burner and are usually forgotten. Changing ourselves is easy compared to changing other people. Changed people move in a different way, into a new world. However, we live life in a landscape of many people and situations, with rippling effects. Verna's change required things around her to change, also.

## Step Four

The recipe for the Life Plan calls for a timeline to create pressure to help move forward to a specific date. The date is not confined to a set day of the week or month, but is a generalized structure in which to operate. Otherwise, it is easy to use the tomorrow or someday-soon mentality. Timelines force procrastinators to complete goals.

Schedules help organize the way we do business. Once time is scheduled in the daily routine, it's easier to see time as a physical thing. In America's high-speed culture, time is spoken of in terms of something that can be saved, spent, wasted, used or treasured. It is often said that a cell phone, ATM card or some other invention will save us time.

Months and years go by without us using a timeline to make changes and reach goals in our lives. Social paralysis impedes our progress because a deadline isn't imposed as it would be in our employment.

Hawaii was the perfect setting for Verna to impose her own deadline. The diversity of people and their lifestyles opened her to new ways of viewing the world.

Somehow, Verna had assumed that most golfers were intellectually superior to her. However, once she challenged herself to go where, before, she'd never dare go, she didn't feel inadequate. She discovered she had abilities that many of the golf veterans lacked. Most of all, she felt respect.

Verna realized that she could excel anywhere. With her fierce competitiveness, she could hold her own with anyone. For the first time, she saw her past as an asset, if she used it. Until now, she felt sorry for herself and unworthy of success. She had accepted her victim position in life, as where she belonged.

Verna was moving and feeling fluid. Energy rushed in to sweep away negativity that held her back for so many years. Not only did she feel deserving of a good man, she felt pretty. Shedding nine pounds made her feel even better about herself.

Verna was apprehensive about returning home from Hawaii even though she was confident that she was in control of her life. Verna had a new stew cooking on the stove. She wanted to make sure that those at her table had what they needed to grow strong from the nourishment. She changed her original family menu to include too much hot pepper. She wanted to get their attention.

At Verna's 39th birthday celebration dinner, she upset the bellies of her adult children. She passed out copies of her acceptance letter to a university in South Africa, where she would study public health in a country ravaged by AIDS. It was the surprise entree.

Breaking the cycle of family co-dependency went better than Verna expected. The university orientation period and her plane tickets had deadlines that were non-negotiable. Everyone had to go with the flow that Verna put into motion. Her plan had its own momentum and rhythm.

Verna's goal was to be in a loving relationship and have a baby. In most cases, change creates experiences in new territories, thereby bringing new opportunities. Implementing one change produces another.

Verna's life was coming together, in one succulent main course. She felt free to try the new ingredients to cook a masterpiece. Her desire for Mr. Right became secondary to her desire to create a signature recipe.

The South African university was an excellent place for her to try her new and courageous recipe. The final section of her Life-Planning book filled up fast.

# Kicking the Recipe Across the Table
## Get Off Your Ass and Get a Life

1. Do you postpone difficult projects that are important for your personal growth?

2. What was the defining decision/choice at the crossroads of your life that left you changed forever?

3. Recall situations in your life where you lingered too long without significant positive growth.

4. Who or what is the greatest influence in your life? Why?

5. Do you understand why you are where you are?

6. Do you know where you want to be, if you live long enough to reach your 85th birthday?

7. What plans are you implementing to make it happen?

8. Do you have a friend suffering from SP (social paralysis)?

# Mentoring Friends is Like a Pot-Luck Dinner

Relationships with God, family and friends satisfy our need for the primal connection. Not feeling alone is a basic human need. We enter the world attached to an umbilical cord that supplies our needs for months within a warm, soft and protective sack.

Once we're cut away from our mother's cord, we cry. Without being taught, we'll instinctively wrap our fingers around whatever finger is placed in our palm. Seeking connection is an individual journey. Friendship is God's gift to light the way.

The phone was ringing off the hook. I could hear it as I turned the key in the door. It stopped, but started again as I turned the knob to the slam lock.

Breaking my fingernail, on the metal stripping along the side of the door molding, added to the disgust of my homecoming from St. Louis for the New Year. After picking up the phone, I got a click in my ear and then a dial tone. Normally, I don't chase after calls, but I'd missed New Year's Eve night with my baby and was hoping to hear his voice.

Dropping my things on the floor, I headed for the bathroom. I knew that it was the best way to get the caller to call back. I went in, turned on the light and waited. The phone didn't ring. I washed my hands and decided to file down the damaged fingernail.

The bathroom was quiet. Since I was there, I decided to use the toilet. Like clockwork, before I could sit, the phone started up. I caught it on the third ring.

It was Flora and Paschence. Instead of their call, I should have answered nature's call in the bathroom. Flora and Paschence had been at a New Year's Day brunch in my building and wanted to stop by. I hadn't seen them since before Christmas. I blurted out that they could come by and ran to the bathroom for relief.

Paschence entered with a bottle of Jack Daniel whiskey with a green ribbon around the bottleneck. Flora carried a bundle of aluminum foil stuffed in a festive holiday shopping bag. Both women had on short, black dresses and gold/diamond jewelry. Even though dressed similarly, they looked very different. I envied their ten perfectly shaped red nails.

Paschence said, "I'm sorry to barge in on you, but an emergency has come up. I got a lot of nerve just showing up since I never was a member of your talking circle. In fact, I always felt like the circle inside the circle."

"Paschence," I said, "your mommy knew what to name you because you sure try mine."

"I know," she said. "I try to fit in, but it don't always happen."

Flora opened the bottle and found glasses and ice.

"I got some roasted chicken, brown rice with some stir-fried vegetables and rolls," Flora said. "I knew you'd be hungry, coming home to an empty refrigerator."

According to Flora, another neighbor sent the care package along with her love. Flora put the food on a plate then urged Paschence and me to talk. She didn't want to keep me up all night.

If possible, Paschence was too pretty. She had a face that seemed designed by an architect. She had the longest, slender fingers, with nails that never cracked or peeled. Entering a room, she caused people to stare because of her beauty. She looked better at 50 than she had at 30. Her lovers were exclusively white women with money.

Flora's beauty and natural behavior were part of her charm. She settled into my kitchen as if it were her own. While she did, Paschence pumped up for her first serious discussion with me. She never volunteered information. Tonight, because she was going steady with Jack Daniel, she did.

The tray prepared by Flora was magnificent. She brought me a bit of the goodies, displayed on fresh sprigs of mint and basil she found growing in tiny herb pots over my sink. The burgundy and gold place mat matched the holiday ribbon that flowed from the bundle of freshly made breads. My stomach was purring, anticipating the pleasure of finally getting to eat.

Paschence began running her mouth the second I got into my food. She was determined to have her say. Flora was conspicuously quiet, but busy in and out of the kitchen.

On the other hand, Paschence was strangely talkative. My hunger was stronger than my desire to ask questions. Although, I was curious about their late-night visit, I had to eat first.

Paschence said, "Remember when Flora invited you, Ginger and me to Dallas? She was going to her first conference for her new out-of-town job and she wanted our support."

With a full mouth, I nodded to indicate, yes.

"Remember?" Paschence said. "I didn't want to go. You said you couldn't go and Ginger was the only one who said she could go. Remember?"

I nodded and continued to eat.

"Well, Ginger got sick and couldn't go. It fell on me to go with Flora, but I wanted to stay home for Ginger. After days of pressure and feeling guilty, I reluctantly went to Dallas alone with Flora. Remember?"

With her drink, Flora sat on the rug nearby and curled up around the base of the chair. She was quiet, listening to every word Paschence said.

The smell of the food was no longer compatible with the aura in room. I felt an uncomfortable flush of warmth around the back of my arms and at the base of my neck. There was something more happening than a late-night chat among friends.

I stopped eating and sat back. My sixth sense needed to hear the silent pause between spoken words, to tell where truth lay.

"Paschence," I said, "you and Flora didn't come here to tell me what I already know. What's really going on?"

There was heavy foot-dragging as the silence continued until Paschence said, "While I was in Dallas, I was unfaithful to Ginger."

I said, "You had affairs before and you and Ginger went on. What's the big deal?"

"You don't understand," Paschence said. "I thought I was in love, this time."

"In love!" I said. "Give me a break."

Paschence went to the window. She pulled her broad shoulders back and screamed, "I fell in love!"

She turned to us and said, "I had a real love affair!"

This time, silence tiptoed across the hard wood floor without a squeak. For a moment, I thought I had lost the ability to hear. I did feel the unmistakable heavy hearts of Flora and Paschence.

The energy that filled every corner of the room stroked my senses and I felt the gloom everywhere. I was no longer hungry for food, but I was starved for information about the cause of so much sadness.

Trying to make sense out of the connection between the Dallas story and the emotional tension forced me to fight a powerful undertow of mystery. What was so different about Paschence's latest affair, I wondered?

I said, "Paschence, I love you, but you're hardly a saint."

Paschence didn't so much as flinch from my assessment of her. The lack of a reaction made me probe even more, when I said, "White women with money are the only ones who don't get enough of your shit. Is Ginger finally kicking you out?"

Paschence turned to look through the window at the dark, winter sky. Only a whisper of whiskey remained in her glass.

Knowing I was getting closer to an answer to the mystery, I said, "Anyway Paschence, isn't 'love affair' a bit much for a six-day trip?"

After Paschence still didn't respond, I'd had it with her late-night visit only to pose in front of my window.

I said, "In a while, you won't even remember your new lover's name. Look, girl. Ginger's the best relationship you ever had. If you can't get past it, maybe you just have to tell her."

I surrendered to the silence and decided to go through my Christmas gifts, piled near my chair.

Opening my annual St. Louis family box of homemade cookies encouraged Paschence to leave the window and rejoin Flora and I near my overstuffed chair.

My favorite cookies were made of oatmeal, raisins and walnuts. They reminded me of my college years, when a box of cookies from home made whatever was wrong feel better.

Flora, Paschence and me had a smile, as we took a break to nibble.

Feeling more optimistic, I said, "Paschence, a fresh romance can add zest to your relationship. Let the forbidden six days go."

For the first time, with a strange, caustic edge in her voice, Flora added her two cents, "Don't forget the six nights."

"I never wanted to go with you to Dallas, in the first place," Paschence said. "If Ginger hadn't insisted I go, none of this mess would've happened."

Slowly, she slumped to the floor next to the box of cookies and began to pick at the crumbling pieces.

I leaned toward Paschence. With my eyes inches from hers, I asked her, "Why'd you two decide I had to hear all of this soap opera at this hour?"

Flora must have figured I'd reached the limits of my patience. She wet my favorite wine glass with a small corner of Jack Daniel. She spoke softly and said, "You're the only one that can help us out of this serious shit."

I wasn't having it; my last nerve was worked. I said to Paschence, "The worst that can happen is Ginger gets pissed and you have to make nice for a while. Trust me, life will go on."

Paschence let the first shoe fall with the force of something dropped over Hiroshima.

"All that might be true, if I hadn't slept with Fred."

No one in the room breathed.

Flora fought back the tears welling around her eyeliner. Tears and words flooded simultaneously when she said, "I found my husband Fred and Paschence having sex in my house."

That was the second shoe dropping.

Flora couldn't be stopped from telling it all, now. She said, "Paschence, my long-time friend and house guest. I caught her screwing my husband not once, but twice."

I couldn't believe my ears. I said, "Flora. Not Paschence."

Flora started before I even finished talking.

She said, "The first time, I forgot my laptop and had to double back home. On my way to the den, I heard Fred and Paschence's moans and voices coming from the bedroom."

Before continuing, Flora fought to control her breathing.

"I snatched the computer and ran out of the house. It's crazy. Even though it was my husband screwing my girlfriend, *I* felt like the outsider. When the two of them showed up later for the opening of a new, regional office, I decided to pick my time."

Trying to defend herself, Paschence said, "But —"

Flora cut her off and said, "But they didn't give me a chance. I went home and checked my bedroom. The bed was made and I was relieved not to see any signs of being betrayed."

"I didn't betray you, Flora," Paschence said.

Flora shot Paschence a look intended to kill. Instead, it only shut her up so Flora could continue.

Flora said, "A little voice told me to look in the guest room, through the partially opened door. Sound asleep and naked, his left hand, wearing his wedding band, rested on her absurdly slim waist.

There was Fred and Paschence, lying there, so peaceful."

I knew Paschence had a wide streak of freakiness in her. But as Flora's story resonated in my head, I couldn't help but look at Paschence with new eyes.

Flora's intensity narrowed toward her story's finale. When she spoke, it was almost like a vengeful meditation.

Flora said, "I got a pitcher of sweetened tea from the kitchen and filled it with crushed ice. I went back to the bedroom and I emptied it on their naked bodies. They leaped from the bed, screaming like they'd been scalded with the ice."

Without a show of tears, Flora raised her long arms above her head, then wrapped them around her shoulders and began to rock back and forth.

By now, I was standing. All I could do was stare down at Paschence. "You and Fred," I said. "You and your friend's husband. You don't even like men. What the hell was that about?"

Trying to play for sympathy, Paschence said, "I guess you want me out of your place now, right?"

I said, "Flora should've kicked your horny ass and Fred's."

Paschence said, "I know it was wrong." My hands went up to warn Paschence to keep her distance.

I said, "This is so fucked up!" I wanted to slap her stupid.

"I know I fucked up better than anyone," Paschence said. "Please sit back down and hear me out. It's more complicated than sex. You see Flora's here with me, now."

"I'm listening," I said.

Paschence wasted no time trying to make her case. She said, "Fred and I partied and danced like the old Paradise Garage days and my top got sweaty. I wanted to cool off."

"I bet you did," I said.

"One thing led to another and somehow, we ended up in the shower, together," Paschence said. "But no sex happened, just kissing. Later, we went back down to the party, as though nothing happened."

"But something did happen. Didn't it, Paschence?" I said.

Me or nobody else could stop Paschence's story. And to tell the truth, the part of me that wasn't angry wanted her to convince me that she just wasn't a gender-challenged slut.

"The next morning," Paschence said, "after Flora left the house, I went to Fred and we...Fred's the first man to ever kiss me or make love to me. He said things to me I wanted to hear all my life. I still love Ginger, but it's different now."

The only thing missing was the camera crew. This was the place in the movie where music comes up and the scene fades to Flora, the violated wife, who has her say.

On cue, Flora said, "In a strange way, I was glad it happened. I'd planned to ask Fred for a divorce."

I was caught by surprise. I said, "I didn't think things were that bad between you and Fred."

Flora shrugged her shoulders and said, "Here I was worried how to tell Fred about a younger man, without crushing his ego, and there he was turning out a life-long lesbian."

Flora lay on the floor and laughed from deep inside. Meanwhile, Paschence swished her finger around as a stirrer in her drink and licked a few drops from her fingertip. She swung herself toward Flora and said, "Don't laugh at me, Flora. I got the same plumbing as you."

Flora said, "That's the problem. You could've had the most beautiful men and babies in the world, if you wanted."

I said, "Ladies, we need to think this through. Flora, do you want a divorce from Fred?"

"Yes," Flora said. "I love Fred. I just can't be married to him, anymore. Will you help us end it all without bitterness?"

I said, "You two blind-sided me, but, yes. Of course, I will. Just give me a few days to prepare."

Paschence said, "*Your* blind side! What about me? Since I was born, no man or boy ever turned me on."

Jet lag was getting the best of me, but I was determined to get the last word in before I put them out.

"Paschence, sometimes the message has got to have the right messenger. Anyway, at our age, there's little that's completely new. Even so, the right presentation throws a new light on old things and makes them new.

Flora, any man you screw after Fred all these years is going to feel like love. Don't jump so fast. Stand up for your feelings in your marriage before you do it outside of it. Your young minister will get to know the same Flora who left Fred.

And Paschence, you need to think about why you said you'd never become a fat cow by getting pregnant. That's pure vanity. You avoided being a woman all your life. You won't learn to cook, iron or do your own nails and hair. Women keep you and let you play mommy with their children. Now after some strapless dick, you swear your old ass is in love. Give me a fucking break!"

Being full of whiskey made Paschence bold. Her body grew rigid with indignation. She slurred a little when she shouted, "Who you talking to?"

"To a sneaky lesbian so low she fucks her friend's husband!"

If Paschence was wounded, she recovered quickly. She said, "You're judging me? At least my female lovers are faithful. That's more than I can say for the men you pick."

Flora leaped to her feet. She looked at Paschence and me standing face to face. She tried to will some civility into the room. Her long, thick arms closed around us in a tender semi-circle.

As Paschence dried tears streaking down her cheeks with the edge of a dinner napkin, Flora gently rocked us, both.

Inside the circle, I whispered, "In the last twenty-four hours, I've been in two airports in two different cities. I believe marriage is sacred and I believe in loyalty between friends. Right now, I'm too tired to help anybody, not even myself."

As though signaling an end to a boxing match, the phone rang. I let the message service pick up.

I said, "Don't come to my door this late with bullshit, again. Bad news can wait until morning. All I can do is carry the burden through the night in my bed. You two get your stuff and get out of here."

After Flora and Paschence left, I picked remains of food out of the aluminum foil. My broken fingernail still needed filing. My body needed rest. I thought about myself for a minute.

Since my college romance, marriage and divorce two years later, I was guilty of selecting men that were marriage proof.

But, now, I eagerly anticipate hearing from the man in my life. God slowed me down with enough pain and grief to open my heart to receive my personal messenger of love.

" and ye shall know the truth and the truth shall make you free."

(John 8: 32)

# Kicking the Recipe Across the Table
## Mentoring Friends is Like a Pot-Luck Dinner

1. Do friends excessively depend on you to listen to their problems?

2. Do you respond to needy friends or do you avoid them?

3. Do you feel you have to help friends in trouble?

4. Is your maturity important when you lend a shoulder to unhappy friends?

5. Do you keep secrets that, if revealed, could harm a friend?

6. How far do friends go to help you?

7. Is it possible to be too helpful?

8. Do you listen as much as you talk?

# Baking Sticky Buns

When I came home from a speaking engagement, Fred sat reading the paper in the lobby. His face lit up when he saw me. He rescued me by relieving me of the burden of my computer, flip chart and visual aids.

"Because of you, Fred, I got hardly any sleep last night. I'm sure you know why."

"I don't know what you're talking about," Fred said, as he reached for the elevator button.

"Flora didn't tell you she was at my place, last night?"

"She couldn't tell me anything. I moved out. I'm at my brother's."

"You and your brother together, again? There's not a woman safe in the whole city."

"Safer than you think. Kenny's fat and bald, and he wears bifocals."

The elevator came and we hustled on. Fred was still a damn good-looking man. His gray hair didn't detract from his youthfulness. His streetwise style and suave manner still gave him at least one admirer. If Flora let Fred get away, she was out of her natural mind.

Once inside the sequence of locks, I shoved the lecture material into a stall in the hall closet. I gave Fred the menu to a neighborhood restaurant and stirred him toward the phone.

The Upper Westside restaurant menu was thicker than a small-town phone book. As Fred looked over the food list before ordering, he got the message that after a hard day's work, I had no intention of cooking, particularly since he was there for a therapy session.

"I'd love me some Spanish food," Fred said, nearly salivating over the menu.

"The only thing Flora cooks is soul food. Order what you want. When Flora gets here, at least you won't have to negotiate what to eat."

Fred said, "She's not coming."

"What?"

"She said she told you the whole story and you were more for me than for her."

"I'm not for one of you over the other, that's unprofessional. And there's no way in hell I approve of you cheating on her with Paschence."

"I got busted in bed with her girlfriend, in her house," Fred said. "I'm lucky she didn't kill me. If she had, at least it meant she still cared."

"I'm glad she didn't kill you. If she had, you couldn't ask for fresh avocado salad with yellow rice with whatever you order for me, please."

I called Flora and left her a message to come by, no matter what time she came in. Flora had a lot of nerve ducking a meeting she set up — a lot of nerve or cowardice.

I filled the kettle with water for tea. Whenever I'm at a loss for what to do or say, I start boiling water. A whistling tea kettle is like a timer for my thoughts. The build up to a loud whistle soothes me until the final Jeopardy question forces me to come up with an answer.

Fred sat on a stool and I stood at the stove, in my bare feet. I was still dressed in my presentation clothes, with the "Hello My Name Is" sticker still on my blouse. Draped across another stool was my presentation hair.

I had worn a mid-length wig. My theatre background, you know. Speaking in front of people is still a bit of theatre. The ham in me still loved the attention.

I started wearing braids in 1972. Straightened hair never agreed with me and I have the bald spots to prove it. But dressing in a costume, to play whatever part life calls for, was always something I could do.

As Fred and I waited for the food to be delivered, he said, "I remember you doing Summer Stock Theatre out in Missouri, years ago. You were good on stage."

"I always enjoyed finding my character," I said.

Fred put my wig on his head and said, "Maybe I could star as my female character. Then I could crush men to get my way and cry when I they don't let me."

"Don't be too good at it, Fred. You might not make it back," I said. "Why would any man want to be a woman?"

"Then I could destroy men and still be the victim."

Fred walked around, switching his hips. The more I laughed, the more he exaggerated his fake female stroll.

He put his hands on his hips and whipped his neck back and forth. With his hands on his hips, Fred whipped his neck from side to side and said, "And believe me child, sister wouldn't take no mess."

Thank God for the doorbell. The food came before Fred needed a bikini wax.

Because of tension about what was to come, Fred and I ate like the Last Supper. The king of king's fish came with bell peppers, onions and tomatoes in an olive oil sauce, over yellow rice. There was hot basil, garlic with black beans and sweet plantains on the side. The meal came with my favorite avocado salad.

Fred and I would talk, sure we would. But he and Flora's problem wasn't going anywhere. We had time to savor our food before I dove into trying to resolve a bitterness that took years to create.

And if not a resolution, there was always the dream of elusive closure. To come anywhere near that sacred animal, Flora had to be at the next session.

I lied to Fred when I told him I was neutral between he and Flora. I'm human; I took his side. My objectivity about them as a couple was clouded by my empathy for Fred.

I was disappointed with both of them, but I was angry with Flora. However, I realized I was guilty of harboring feelings about women passed down through generations, about how a woman is always at fault, somehow, when a man strays.

Fred was wrong. Still, I was grateful that Flora stayed away and allowed me a chance to put my biased thoughts on a shelf so high, I'd need a ladder to reach them.

Twenty-four hours had passed since I found out about the shattered marital bonds of two of my closest friends. I needed more time to ponder an effective response to the cheating between a husband and wife.

Unfairly, I saw Flora as the catalyst for the sordid, bed-hopping episodes in Dallas. It was her decision to leave New

York and her family to chase a career that set in motion a Texas-sized drama.

## Coming to Terms with "Truth"

Days passed before I got the principals together. To create a warm atmosphere, I cooked a pot of turkey soup. I discovered long ago that the smell of food cooking encouraged cooperation.

My pot of soup was full of fresh carrots, zucchini, red and green bell peppers, plum tomatoes, sliced leeks and white Spanish onions with lots of Italian parsley.

Fred gave Flora some peasant bread with grated Parmesan cheese from the round, crusty loaf. The large oval pasta bowl was steaming hot and bellowed its herbal aroma. Fred and Flora each got a soup bowl and dug in.

I didn't eat with them. Almost ignored, I observed their interaction and listened to them talk about their children, Naomi and Little Fred. They were having a routine dinner until Fred finished the last bit of his bread. The time had come for the serious work that was overdue.

I cleared the table and loaded the dishwasher. Flora sat on the floor near my favorite chair. Fred stayed in his chair. I moved to the living room and pulled Fred by the hand. I directed him to sit on the couch. We were as ready as we would ever be.

I said, "Let's all hold hands and pray for guidance."

With our bodies nourished, we prayed until a peace came over the room.

"Fred. Flora," I said. "Is your marriage so damaged that you can't love each other, again?"

They looked in each other's eyes. Maybe it was because their "no's" sounded like "I do's," but we three laughed and whatever remaining tension sprang from the room.

"Now, can we work with no one in mind except the two of you?"

Flora said, "I don't have a problem seeking help, but Fred does." She cast her eyes toward the floor and said, "For years, I asked you to really talk to me, Fred. I just got tired hearing my own voice."

Fred leaned forward with elbows on both of his knees, his hands clasped together. With commitment, he said, "I'm here, now and I'm ready."

My energy was high after my cooking therapy session, so I offered a suggestion.

I said, "Flora, why don't you get a cushion for yourself."

Fred tossed her one from the couch.

"I've been dealing with your conflict for a whole week. I hope, now, you both realize the consequences of your actions."

I'm sure Flora nodded; I think Fred did.

"Let's work on getting you two to communicate and saving what's left of your marriage," I said.

Their faces were eager, but uncertain. From manila envelopes, they took out notepads with responses to questions I'd asked them to answer before coming by.

"You start, Fred. And no negotiating, OK?"

Fred read from his list of questions. "Why'd I marry her? Flora's everything I wanted. When she married me, that's when my life started."

Unblinkingly, I stared at Flora. After a moment, she knew what I wanted from her. As her nervous fingers squeezed her sweat-dampened notepad, she said, "Why did I marry Fred?"

Flora hugged the notepad to her breast. She exhaled like a long dormant volcano and said, "I loved Fred from the time I met him at a party and looked into his movie-star handsome face."

After looking momentarily stunned, Fred pushed back, sat on the couch and crossed his legs. He glanced at his notepad and back and Flora. While Flora and I waited, Fred repeated the action twice more before refusing to look up from the page.

With great difficulty, Fred said, "Why...Paschence?"

Then his pleading eyes latched onto Flora's. He said, "Paschence and I were drowning in the same river. It wasn't love, wasn't even about sex. We used each other to save ourselves from a death we couldn't face."

With eyes only for Fred, Flora listened, for the first time in a long time.

Fred got up and paced the room like a long-distance runner cooling down. Finding his stride at the end of the race, he said, "OK, OK, hear it is. I was terrified of getting old. I was falling apart and in my own house, it wasn't even news."

In profile, Fred looked out the window. He stood, unable or unwilling to give up the floor. Flora looked at him like he was a banner headline and all the news.

Fred said, "Paschence was a priest to my confession of fears. For her, I wasn't a father or husband defending my failures, I was just a man." Fred could not sit down.

On the floor near Fred's feet, her eyes moist, Flora sat like concerned royalty. Finally, she looked at me and I nodded at her.

Flora glanced at the next question on her sheet of paper. She said, "Why Reverend Callister?"

Flora stood up and read her answer directly to Fred.

"David Callister's devoted to me," she said. "He knows what I need almost before I do. David's the best thing that's happened to me in a long time."

Fred screamed at Flora and said, "The reverend lay healing hands on you or just lay you?"

Flora lurched at Fred and said, "The only thing to stop you and Paschence from screwing in my house is you ran out of rooms!"

The passion Flora and Fred faced each other with was turned inside out. Fred stalked into the kitchen to chew a crust of bread. He was really there to cool off.

While Fred was gone, Flora wiped her eyes and went into the bathroom. She returned with a wet washcloth she used to wipe her face. She was having a hot flash.

Later, as we agreed, Fred and Flora each vented for a half-hour, unleashing years of pain. They calmed down by degrees, like 2-year-olds after a tantrum.

Flora dabbed the neatly folded washcloth against her face and throat. She placed it on a ceramic coaster near her discarded written statements. She was breathing hard, now that it was all out in the open.

Truth was set free, but neither Fred nor Flora was exorcised of the demons: jealousy and envy. Dying love can be smelled a lifetime away from two people destined for a romantic fall.

The fate of my friends' relationship teetered on a mountain's edge. It could go either way. The time came for a power greater than my own. Devine love had to make it right.

For the second time that night, the three of us held hands. Invoking the greatest power, we held hands and repeated the Lord's Prayer.

Our circle was close. I smelled the saltiness of Flora's beaded sweat and the perfume scent of a trickle winding down the cleavage of her breasts.

From the warm kitchen, branches of mint, sage and basil in my herbal pots mingled our senses with the comfort of home.

A last "Amen" sent Fred and Flora to sit on the couch. With felt-tip markers and my flip chart, we began to chart the trail of effects and causes that led to their communication breakdown and nearly the end of a marriage.

Flora and Fred were terrified of losing each other and ready to submit to the process of recovering the pieces of broken trust.

I was glad to step out of the referee role and back into that of communication consultant. It was a hell of a lot less stressful and way more productive.

Finally, it was time to identify the problems that they felt needed to be addressed, so they could begin to repair their marriage.

# Flora's Perception of Fred's Shortcomings

- Lacks dependable money for household expenses
- Works for himself and refused good paying jobs
- Large debt
- Grand ideas on zero budget
- Unorganized business ventures
- Used by friends and family
- Keeping secrets
- Seldom home for dinner or family activities on time
- Infrequent and short, uninteresting sex
- Sex without foreplay or romantic time
- Does not dance, anymore
- Too much television, e-mail, telephone time
- Failure to initiate exciting dates/nights out
- Unappreciative in general
- Usually late
- Friends come before family
- Drinks too much and then talks loud

# Fred's Perception of Flora's Shortcomings

- Gets extremely angry about the smallest thing
- Wants to be in charge
- Expects me to admit I'm wrong when I'm not
- Is always right
- Waits for me to fail so that she can say she told me so
- Is gaining too much weight
- Corrects me in front of other people
- Talks when I'm talking
- Shares our personal business with her family and friends
- Does not know a first down from a first inning
- Very little spontaneous, passionate sex
- Lets me know she does not need me
- Stays angry for long periods of time
- Will not submit to my final word about anything

Flora and Fred looked at the list of comments as though they were about people they didn't know. They saw themselves differently and were shocked by what they believed about each other. Fortunately, they did not defend or deny.

Now that we had taken a chance on each other and trusted each other to work toward reconciliation, the rest of the battle would be helping Fred and Flora design communication techniques that worked for them.

## Communication Needs

### Fred

Fred needed Flora to respect him as a man in their marriage. He expected Flora to accept him as the traditional head of the household, as she said she wanted when they married.

However, for Flora to defer to Fred, he had to make her know that she was emotionally and economically secure with him. For him, of course, respect was the most pressing problem he needed addressed.

### Flora

Flora needed Fred to willingly share his professional and private life with her, so she could be a part of his world. Flora needed more intimacy. In order for Fred to include her and be more sexually attracted to her, Flora knew she had to stop her constant complaining.

Flora was aware of her habit of constantly pointing out Fred's faults, in an effort to reduce his importance as a man and to increase her importance as a woman. Like most women, she needed to be needed.

## Communicating Forgiveness in a Relationship

Flora and Fred reaffirmed their commitment to being married. Step one was deciding to preserve the relationship, no matter what their sins. Once two people decide to remain a couple, everything else can be organized around making them whole, again.

Fred and Flora apologized to each other. They said they were sorry for their extra-marital relationships. For Flora, Fred's apology didn't make her forget he and Paschence in bed, together. Neither did her apology to Fred make images of Reverend Callister disappear. However, it is where forgiveness starts. Confessing wrongdoing was step two.

Step three is the acid test and can cause more pain than the wrongdoing, itself. Neither Fred nor Flora were to mention the other's adultery, again.

Never bringing up the past as a weapon against each other is the hard part. Progressing past this point takes time, but eventually there must have a cut-off date. To expect one to never bring it up is unrealistic.

However, venting hurt can alleviate the anger. A mutually agreed upon cut-off date, ends the habit of bringing it up at all. Honest closure is essential.

At this juncture, the relationship's success or failure will become evident. If Fred and Flora continued to do "retro-communication" and couldn't go forward, their lives would be stuck in the past.

Seasoned Women and seasoned men in long-term relationships, find ways to stay together and weather the worst things imaginable.

# Kicking the Recipe Across the Table
## Baking Sticky Buns

1. When you know both people, is it possible to offer objective advice?

2. Can a platonic friendship exist between a  married man and a single woman?

3. Can friendship survive a sexual betrayal with a common friend?

4. Do you value trust between friends?

5. Can forgiveness overcome pain caused by human faults?

6. Does maturity enable greater acceptance of misconduct and going forward?

7. When friends are in trouble, do you feed the fire or try to put it out?

8. Does anger have a place between friends when one or both feels mistreated?

9. Can anger end, if one friend feels unfairly treated?

# Options for Living

*"All you get is time to live, but
the big question is deciding how to use it."*

## Relationships Between Women

Sexual relationships between Seasoned Women and seasoned men are usually the focus of my writing. As a heterosexual woman who grew up in a conventional Christian home, I'm biased about what is normal.

As you may have gathered by now, I consider unions between men and women to be the components for human reproduction and the reason we exist. Of course, there will be those who disagree with me, but I can only advocate and support what I honestly believe.

I apologize to those who feel I'm excluding them from merely being, as we all are, human and ones who experience what we all feel, if we're lucky — the love of and for another soul.

Seasoned Lesbian Women and seasoned gay men are children of God and, as such, deserve love and respect. However, it is my lack of understanding of same-sex relationships that pushes me to remain open to different ways of living in society.

It is toward such an understanding that I openly discuss lesbian relationships in this book. Not to do so would be unthinkable in a world that has, with notable exceptions, come around to thinking that same-sex relationships shouldn't be condemned or its principals persecuted, but be accepted as part of the grand mosaic of which humanity is composed.

Indeed, many of you are my friends while others are clients whom I see personally and/or professionally. I, both, care about and love you. So how could you not be included, here?

## Traditional Views of Sexuality

There seems to be more transforming medical procedures today than there are people on which to perform them. However, for the most part, the biology of the male and female is fixed and used to do what bodies are designed to do — create sperm to fertilize eggs. I hope it's safe to assume that you know who, of the male and female, supplies which.

While same-sex couples can't have children in the traditional way, they are able to form loving relationships and when found acceptable candidates for parenting, adopt children. The bonds formed by people aren't solely determined by the anatomy they possess at birth. The close ties are influenced by internal factors, like emotions and feelings for those who, through some magnetic chemistry, attract the other.

Throughout time, women from many social and ethnic groups have been lovers to other women. These sisters of Sappho have been scorned and branded outcasts.

Until the 1960s, most lesbians kept a low profile. They suffered through ill-conceived marriages, bore children and raised families that eventually made them grandmothers and great grandmothers.

They remained in loveless relationships with men because of intolerance and prejudice or found a kind of love with men that suppressed, but never quite buried, their desire for other women.

Some of these women still aren't open about their love because of some residual societal prejudice. They face family pressures to conform and be "normal."

In spite of high-profile lesbians coming out in prime time, as did Ellen DeGeneris and Rosie O'Donnell after her go at being a daytime talk show host, there are still many women who suffer from an agoraphobia that has to do with coming out.

## Trend Setters

The women of my generation are warriors and sheroes. Our population experienced radical social and moral revolutions firsthand. We lived during a time when homosexuality was despised as much as Negroes.

We know the harsh consequences of alternative lifestyles that turn upside down what conservative society believes. There was (and many would argue, still are) women who battle to pierce the glass ceiling in jobs, even without the scarlet letter "L" for being a lesbian, in the workplace.

Open lesbian behavior threatens many purported heterosexuals, no matter what the law says about equal treatment. Societal values are slower to change than laws. It can't be proved, but the nation's acceptance of homosexuality might be greater had the white, gay rights leadership aligned themselves with the Civil Rights movement. Personally, I'd be more of an advocate, if gays had been more openly supportive of the political phenomenon upon which the legal protection of same-sex relationships was built, namely, the Civil Rights movement.

In the 1950s, gays were not the bold fighters they are, today. They weren't truly galvanized until 1969, when many of them were bashed and brutalized in the Greenwich Village incident known as the Stonewall Riot.

While many Civil Rights movement insiders knew the Reverend Martin Luther King's protest strategist Bayard Rustin was gay, nobody who participated in the struggle in Selma or Birmingham, Alabama identified themselves as gay people. If they entered the fray for the rights of Black folks, they checked their sexual affiliation at the door. The dogs, water hoses, clubs and the KKK cooled many passions in search of equal rights.

A segment of the gay population greatly benefits from the laws they have recently mobilized to demand. Somehow, I can't help thinking of their playing it safe when babies, young people and the old paid in blood for fair and equal treatment under the law.

With such a personal memory of history, you can imagine the lively discussions I have with my seasoned homosexual friends, when they tell me about their civil rights.

It doesn't take a Nostrodamas to predict that the coming decades will see Seasoned Women vying for male companionship in a shrinking male population. Already, women are beginning to live with other women in some most interesting arrangements.

These are bold women who don't fear showing their affection for each other as life partners. Hopefully, not throwing stones themselves, these new-age women are crashing through glass ceilings of a different kind.

There are female couples over 50 that I've known for years who have lived secretly as lovers. Some are retired and now living in small, suburban communities while others live in large cities.

"With income from investments, I do pretty good," Paschence said.

I said, "What about your girl Ginger?"

Paschence said, "Ginger's self-employed. After she retires next October, we're going to New Mexico and look for a place."

I watched Paschence pull her hair back from her face as she smoked a cigarette. She noticed how I watched her and smiled before putting the cigarette out.

She said, "You know I only smoke when water is wet. Other than that, I don't smoke."

As Paschence fanned the last cloud of smoke away, we laughed like a couple of schoolgirls caught lighting up in the restroom. Only, she was the freshman trying to be cool, while I was way past that.

"Why New Mexico?" I said. "It's so far."

"From what?" she said.

Once she put it that way, I had to scramble for something that made sense.

"Everybody here knows you. And Ginger loves it here," I said.

"Not so much as you think," Paschence said. "Ginger and me are looking for a retirement paradise. Why can't it be New Mexico?"

Ginger had been widowed in her early twenties by the death of a rich real estate developer. She had a grown daughter in California and managed commercial properties.

Paschence's and Ginger's income guaranteed them a comfortable retirement, as long as Ginger's breast cancer stayed in remission.

Many Seasoned Women reach a point in life where they must decide on a living arrangement that determines the quality of life for the balance of time that remains.

Once past 50, marriages often fall apart and the nest is empty of children. Women usually survive their parents, husbands, male siblings and friends. Not surprisingly, women who rely on the company of other women later in life are becoming more commonplace. It's done not only for physical reasons, but for practical ones, as well.

Economic security and the serenity it brings is the goal for many women of my generation. In order to continue the high standard of living that includes travel, shopping and trips to the hair and nail salon, Seasoned Women are creating a new (as the Noel Coward play is called) "design for living."

Most heterosexual marriages and committed relationships that occur after age 50 combine the best features of both lives. Same-sex relationships offer the same advantages as traditional ones.

## Ultimate Symbiosis

Seasoned Women who pool their resources create a home that yields rewards beyond financial security. The mature female union provides equality and often benefits each woman who has weathered life and, as a result, is at her best. Within the relationship, a male role may exist, but it is usually acted out by a female knowledgeable of the mistakes actual men make.

Everyone needs a good wife, including a woman. However, the traditional Christian marriage has no place for the woman to have a wife. In reality, the quality of her life would greatly improve, if she also had a wife, as her husband does in her.

The role of mother/wife is awesomely self-sacrificing. By age 50, after some thirty years of marriage, the woman is whipped. If a career was pursued simultaneously, she is even more overwhelmed.

No wonder during mid-life crises, husbands think they need a young girl to re-ignite their libido. It's not that his wife has lost the pepper from her hot sauce, she just needs what he got for thirty years or more from her — a full-time housekeeper, nanny, interior decorator, nurse, accountant and lover on demand.

Nurturing wives bring more to a relationship than sex. Although the familiar image is of an aging wife, suffering at home in the wake of her aging husband balling it up with a sexy young thing, there are some long-term advantages to a husband who stays in a committed relationship. Studies show that these men live longer than their youth-chasing counterparts.

## Who Needs Whom

While statistics show that men live longer when married (no, it doesn't just seem longer), women live longer than men with or without husbands. Large numbers of Seasoned Women will attend a former husband's funeral with the other woman present. These mourners will often sit in separate pews, the connection between them veiled in silence.

According to the United States Census Bureau, concerning the older population report of March 1999, women vastly outnumber men among older adults.

In 1999, 24.7 million men and 30.6 million women were age 55 and over, a male-female ratio of 81 to 100. With age, the male portion of the ratio steadily dropped.

For the 64-year-old age group, the ratio was 92 to 100 and in the group 85 years and over, men plummeted to a ratio of 49 to 100.

# Living Arrangements —
# Married to Being Forever Single

Most of us in the seasoned age group came of age during the free-love era of the 1960s. Young people threw off the sexual conservatism of earlier generations.

Both sets of my grandparents had very conservative households, as did my parents. I am the only one of my siblings to get divorced. Since divorce is so alien to my family, they had to venture reasons for my failure at it.

Mother blamed my New York lifestyle while daddy blamed the theater and the way being a part of it shaped me. Well, I was there. I blame nothing more sinister than my own lack of maturity.

The 1960s was a wild backdrop to being young. We pushed life to the limit. If it could be ingested, inhaled or debated until someone saw the light and agreed with you, it was worth every moment — that is, of course, until the agonizing reappraisals demanded a price for the permissiveness that was rampant.

The institution of marriage took a beating. It was all about unrestricted freedom for the individual and to hell with cultural traditions. Large segments of the young got lost finding themselves. Some young-married searchers deserted their spouses for the trip.

Doing your own thing became a matter of racial or sexual choice. It was an open-door society that let everything in uncensored. With eagle-eyed hindsight, I see that the decade of the 1960s was the beginning of a gulf between the generations that time has only widened.

My generation's great efforts to bring about basic human rights for the underdogs of society is something for which we can always be proud, but we made a lot of mistakes, too. We'd do well to remember that, when our nostalgia becomes failed memory.

With all the assaults on marriage over the years, it still stands as a time-tested institution whose endurance can be pitted against any other cultural phenomena you can name. There must be some undeniable logic and sense to it. It has outlasted so many experiments to find a better way to perpetuate humanity.

However much we embrace marriage now, there was a period when it became passé. I remember when my friend Joyce got married. It was a lovely outdoor ceremony and I was thrilled to be attending a ritualistic celebration of love.

The reception area was filled with guests who were mutual friends excited to be reunited after many years of separation. It was as if we cherished a beautiful reminder of committed love. The unrestrained partying at the wedding reception was a flashback to the good old days.

In the way so much of life goes in cycles, weddings became popular, again. I have many single and divorced seasoned friends who, after years of avoiding it like spills on a white suit, got married. Still, there are large numbers of women who only attend weddings as a guest or bridesmaid.

Here are some statistics on the Marital Status and Living Arrangements: March 1998 (Update) prepared by Terry A. Lagaila, United States Census Bureau, Division of Population.

In 1998, 110.6 million adults (56.0 percent of the adult population) were married and living with a spouse.

Among people age 25 to 35 years old, 13.6 million had never been married, representing 34.7 percent of all people in that age group.

The proportion of married couples that identified the woman as the householder (head of household) has tripled since 1990 from 7.4 percent in 1990 to 22.9 percent in 1998.

Nearly half (45.2 percent) of women 65 years old and over were widowed. Of the elderly widows, 70.1 percent lived alone.

## Women Who Never Married

Many Seasoned Women have lived their entire life unmarried. Their numbers are much higher than you might imagine. Women in this group have many reasons for not marrying.

Most of these women I spoke to were not opposed to being married, but they would only do so if they found the right man. Their stand on the matter was that they would not settle for a man who they saw as less than they deserved.

Setting scientific standards aside, in my survey I found a small number of single seasoned women who had refused proposals of marriage (not more than 47 out of 210 women asked). The majority had never received a serious marriage proposal and approximately 12 were asked but the wedding never happened, for one reason or another.

Not all women prefer men as marriage partners, choosing instead to live with another woman. However the vast majority of women I surveyed preferred a male partner as a husband.

There is, unfortunately, a large number of young women of marrying age who would be wonderful mothers and mates to husbands, that is if they chose to get married. However, they are delaying having children and avoid domesticity with equal determination. Others have decided to not ever have children.

Unlike the women of my age group who failed to connect with Mr. Right in their prime, younger women tell me that they're happy being single. It appears that many of them, as successful career women, have opted for the single lifestyle that was once thought to be the bitter returns of a woman who couldn't have it all.

## The Single-Life Attraction

The single life is certainly an alternative to nest building and it appears to be gaining momentum as a trend. From my experiences with young women and older, post-menopausal women, many of their weekends begin with a happy hour at a popular bar or dinner and drinks in a familiar restaurant, or a stop by the video store and a call out for home-delivered food.

For some of my female peers, a great deal of dead time is filled with hey-girlfriend-what's-up phone calls. It confirms the existence of at least one other aging human being who is alone. The telephone becomes a lifeline, which flips the statement from the phone company commercial: It's not like being there. It's like not being where you are, alone.

The Internet, pagers and cell phones are major components for those who try to stave off the isolation of living in a world full of people where, incredibly, loneliness is rampant. Then without realizing it, women who carefully purchase the latest communication devices have their own behavior preoccupied with accessing information between those same devices. No face to face talk. No pressing of the flesh, but lots of busy tech work, alone.

Singles' parties and the club scene quickly become boring, after awhile. You see the same mature people at the same old places, doing the same Electric Old Slide for those who Cha-Cha real smooth. And it may be that those who raise their hands in the air and wave them like they just don't care are trying to signal for something new.

Either way, partying with the graying crowd or playing the in-house recluse is only an attempt at filling time. Others find traveling and immersing themselves in doing craftwork a way to busy the devil's workshop.

However, none of these pursuits equal the satisfaction of being in a close relationship with another person who has your back as well as your heart and, hopefully, a few other organs.

Seasoned Women should at least stay open for a potential partner. They shouldn't too quickly close the door on someone who may not appear to be Mr. Right, but who could be, with greater acceptance, Mr. As Is.

For as long as there has been aging, women have learned that longevity is a miraculous agent for instilling tolerance for what other people are, as opposed to the young who focus on what people are not.

## Androgyny: A Choice of Circumstance

I have a major problem with the current generation's infatuation with choosing to live happily without a man/husband. Of course, we're all individuals and only have, as the soap opera's billed "one life to live," but a culture that encourages not having a mate may have to depend on the pool of adopted children to preserve it.

And I must be clear that I'm not knocking the humane act of bringing home children abandoned by life. However, without people actively involving themselves in the less than Norman

Rockwell or Cosby*esque* joys of parenting, we're left to depend on children who resulted from a deposit without a return.

Many mentoring women encourage young women to be happy by striving for self-fulfillment. They aren't so inclined to advise women on how to prepare for being in a successful relationship, where bearing children in an intact family is the expectation.

There should be a midpoint between the two, some balance that gives value to each and an acknowledgement that each may be appropriate for different times in a woman's long life.

Mentoring women should be aware that a stronger influence on their advisees is what they do more than what they say. If a mentor is, herself, living a life of independence, devoid of a man and romance, she may be teaching by example.

A Seasoned Woman gets her props from younger, impressionable women for their job title, attire, address and the perception of comfort. Not only do the younger women take our advice and use our network to advance careers, they also observe all that is available for them to see. Our attitudes toward men is a part of our complete picture presentation. Our spoken words concerning men can burn imprints into young minds, so be mindful of hateful language and attitudes toward men.

Seasoned Women shouldn't allow the choice to remain single in our 50s and 60s to influence younger women to do the same. If Seasoned Women have been married, widowed and parents by this time, it would suggest to younger women that being alone, after living a traditionally involved life, is simply a result of circumstances.

A Seasoned Woman, whose glamour and evidence of success may give younger women an unreal image, has an obligation to mentor and promote a balanced life for them. Many of us are not as happy being single as we appear to be.

The yin and yang are complete statements of life. They are ancient Chinese symbols of the harmony and balance between unified men and women.

There seems to be an unconscious attitude that a woman hasn't had the total life experience if she doesn't experiment with androgyny. The trend to be both male and female pushes them into an unhealthy place, for herself and community. The healthy growth of a community is dependent upon its people. Having thousands of unmarried women choosing to remain single and childless is no way to push a community forward.

As far as I was able to observe, women in the 1990s opted for being complete without the need for anyone else. Even women's language is influenced by how they see their position in relation to men.

For example, women often say of having a man who can do nothing for them, "I can do bad by myself" or "I don't need a man to validate my womanhood," and "what's love got to do with it."

These expressions communicate a negative attitude toward men. They show the uncompromising attitude of the liberated, financially secure woman toward men.

Language promotes attitude and attitude promotes behavior. The popularity, today, of the androgynous woman encourages a mindset in women to have babies whenever, however and with whomever they chose.

For women who bought into what I call the syndrome of androgyny, getting impregnated by the right man's sperm to give her baby the traits she admired was the mission.

The sperm-donating man could be married, single or gay, as long as he could make the perfect baby for her to rear, alone. These women planned to raise the child without the financial and emotional support from the father. The relationship with the man was anticipated to be a hassle.

The idea that a woman elects to become the sole breadwinner and sole childcare provider — in effect, both father and mother — has become more acceptable. Many women never identify the biological father.

The 1998 United States Census Reports in Population Characteristics that: about 19.8 million children under age 18 live with one parent (27.7 percent of all children under age 18).

Children who lived only with their father were more likely to be living with a divorced father (44.4 percent) than with a father who never married.

The majority of children who lived with a single parent in 1998 lived with their mother (84.1 percent).

Approximately 40.3 percent of these children lived with mothers who were never married.

The women of the 1990s have set themselves up to be androgynous. The encouragement of Seasoned Women to focus on their self-development has frequently pushed them too far toward androgyny. As mature women, we have been too successful in encouraging female autonomy.

Now, we are stuck with the fall-out we set in motion. If we continue to remain silent about it, we might be responsible for a younger generation of women growing older in unhealthy, self-imposed isolation. We need grandchildren who are products of homes with both sets of parents.

If the popularity of life led single persists, there'll be few mergers of in-laws into an extended family network for us to share as we age as grandparents. The quality of our final years depends on the family units that are sustained, today. Our clocks are ticking to become grandparents too, so that we can enjoy a balanced family structure.

The over-glamorized 1990s' campaign for being single and proud will be corrected. Unlike many other American women, Black women historically have had to be independent. Therefore, they need to be careful about buying into concepts that can further isolate them from their men.

As further reported in the 1998 United States Census: of 25- to 34-year-old people representing all groups who had never been married (34.7 percent), Blacks represented (53.4 percent) of this group. More than half of all unmarried people are Black.

Androgyny is a powerfully appealing concept for women who traditionally have been denied equality. Too much masculine or feminine behavior creates disharmony within relationships. Accepting a lifestyle trend that automatically rules out a man to share your dreams leaves a lot to be desired.

At some point, the popularity of female self-sufficiency will probably go the way of the ice box. Self-sufficiency is a choice. Avoiding a relationship with a man will undoubtedly eliminate the need for compromise and the struggle to accommodate another human being into your life, but what is lost has to be carefully measured against what is gained.

## Celibacy and Living Single

Both celibacy and androgyny are self-assigned roles. They are related, but celibacy is an alternative that eliminates sexual contact with a partner. Celibacy has become more popular because of HIV/AIDS, conservative religious teachings and personal choices.

For almost two years, I recently was celibate for a number of reasons. I was under extreme pressures and was overextended, with too little time for myself. It was a perfect time because it was a period between partners. I had no intimate interest in anyone. I wanted to be absolutely left alone. I had to isolate myself emotionally and get quiet.

When you live to be half a century and beyond, you discover that you've incorporated the expectations and unfulfilled promises of generations to whom you owe your very existence and success. You feel an unspoken obligation to try to be what is expected.

Unconsciously, you find yourself trying to live up to a standard of excellence that you don't know how to stop. Since the level of expectations of others never decrease, either you stop and take a break or you'll always drag their inherited baggage with you.

As many of us have experienced, it's difficult when you're the first in the family to accomplish something society considers a milestone achievement. From Vicksburg, Mississippi plantations to a migration to St. Louis, Missouri, it took four hundred years of ancestral slavery to produce my small achievements.

The pride of my grandparents, parents and siblings gives energy to all that I do, but coupled with the arrows slung by life, the load gets harder to bear, after awhile. I can't say it's lonely at the top because I'm still striving, but I do know that pioneers get tired.

I know many peers who are their families' pioneers. We share the joy and responsibility of doing what is correct and expected of us, to the best of our ability. We have been blessed and do not complain. We accept that those to whom much has been given, much is expected.

For those of us who are single, the task of giving back seems endless. We are seen as being in a position to do more than those who have families. And so we do.

I had a close friend who was single, bright and very attractive. She had an excellent position, pretty office and all the professional trappings. When she was near death, I would quietly sit next to her bed, talking to her about all the things we had planned to do, but never got around to because we were too busy.

What saddened me, in addition to her dying, was that she had no husband and no children. There's nothing physical left of her to hold on to except the memories. As long as I can remember, she will be present.

Although single, she never took a vacation. It was always another degree, a special job project and long working hours. Over the past ten years, this has been a recurring phenomenon. Wonderful single women are dying without leaving a biological trace.

I was further affected by my friend's death because, in her fading footprints, I saw myself. I decided to step off the world and let it spin without me, for a while.

Celibacy gave me focus for the specific issues that, as an aging single woman, I needed to resolve. The distraction of sex is eliminated through celibacy. Women need to isolate themselves from sex when they are trying to make objective decisions.

To sort out what to keep and what to get rid of from the closets of your soul and mind takes careful thinking. Outside forces unconsciously affecting you are precisely what you don't need. Give yourself a break.

That sex interferes with the evaluation process of women isn't merely a feeling. If memory serves me right, there is a physiological bonding that happens during sex.

After the male climaxes inside the female, his secretions mix and create a biochemical bonding on the walls of the soft tissue of the uterus. Her system receives his sperm and it stays with her for a while, whether she later becomes pregnant or not.

It is possible that this intimate contact can cause the female's perception of the male to be clouded because her sexual partner has become a part of her system.

Many people are unable to hide an intimate affair because their behavior is different with each other. A woman's demeanor gives her away because the man is, quite literally, in her system.

It is often said that most wives can identify the woman having sex with their husbands because of her behavior in his presence. It is as reliable as fingerprint evidence that a physical bonding has taken place.

It is different for the male. Being outside the body, his penis gland opening is the only way for female secretions to enter his system. Although, after sex a man may feel close to a woman, in the absence of chemical bonding, he is free of emotional attachment. He feels freer to have a variety of sex partners.

For the amount of time a woman chooses, celibacy relieves her of the emotional distractions that she can't easily control as the result of having sex. Her decisions will be made with a cooler head and an undivided heart.

## Solitary Closet Cleaning of the Soul and Mind

I suggest celibacy for every single woman who needs to re-shape her life, even if it's only for a couple of months. You will use the time effectively because you will have time to think about yourself, in isolation. Your energy will be focused solely on you.

Your celibacy should end whenever you feel free to live life on your own terms. When you're ready, you'll take ownership of your life and be ready for what comes next.

My lifestyle changed after my priorities were put in order. Unknowingly, I was preparing myself to become wife material. It wasn't that I didn't have mostly great men in my life from which to choose. Mr. Right was present several times. However, my vision was too dominated by my work to consider a partner with whom to share my life. Also, compromising my freedom was out of the question.

I was divorced at 22 and lived single for 39 years. Being single was a comfortable habit. Being a wife did not occur to me until I met a man I could depend on to take care of me physically, mentally and emotionally. Celibacy allowed me to see him, clearly.

## Marriage as a Viable Option

Why is the viability of marriage worth exploring in depth? The traditional marriage is an institution created to legally support and protect men, women and children in a family unit. It formalizes a legalized commitment between men and women. For many years, it has survived as the best system available to serve the family structure.

More than ever before, our young men and women need each other in a loving marriage for their spiritual and economic stability. Children need the balance that a mother and father provide for healthy growth.

Seasoned Women know that the greatness of the single life is not all it's cracked up to be. Older women know better than anybody that loneliness and being alone are too close to the same thing.

If you observe traveling tour groups, groups of educators, church members, social organizations and casual groups on cruises, bus or train trips, you'll find a larger ratio of mature women to men.

If a viable man sought their company, few of these women would elect to be alone. They would leap at a chance to be with a man, especially in a serious relationship that could lead to marriage. That's real honest girlfriend talk and you know it!

Women who know better must be boldly vocal against the proponents of androgynous living. Positive and negative communications have a ripple effect. Many females unconsciously internalize unproductive messages. Not speaking out against any view of marriage as a dull choice is the most dangerous message of all.

Media are forums where Seasoned Women must begin to do what we did against Jim Crow in the 1960s, watch it and respond to it with action.

Along with the media glitz surrounding the single life, there is the fashionable inclusion of homosexuality as a traditional lifestyle alternative. Slowly, but increasingly, the validation for the homosexual lifestyle is gaining acceptance.

There is a danger that impressionable individuals will unnecessarily adopt lifestyles as a result of people they thought were sincere in their choices, but were looking for a momentary thrill. It's as if Anne Heche played the role of a lesbian with Ellen DeGeneris, then for her next role she chose to portray a heterosexual woman.

Heterosexual women today are facing a shrinking pool of men to marry. If we are to fight trendy notions such as lesbian chic or the self-sufficient woman, we must be more vocal in making our opposition known.

## What to do

What would happen if Seasoned Women led a Heterosexual Pride Day parade every Mother's Day? How about declaring a Heterosexual Pride Month? Let's have advertising touting the return of male/female relationships. We could put signs on the subway or billboards in Times Square that show a man and woman smiling while considering each other. The words on the signs say, "Heterosexuality — the new alternative" or "What a concept!" or "A man and a woman? It just might work."

Imagine Seasoned Women setting aside one day a month to invite a few unmarried young people to their house for a game night such as backgammon, poker, chess or bid whist.

Seasoned Women, our children are limited in their dancing ability. We could sponsor a "Touch-Dancing Night," where we teach them how to dance with a partner without rubbing against each other all night.

Encourage seasoned men to join you in sponsoring a singles' walk for a children's charity and have it culminate in an old-fashioned picnic. It would be a place where the young can mingle, share a meal, play games and sports. By our example, let them learn to have fun outside of sex. Allow them to have examples of respectable behavior demonstrated by seasoned males and females. After all, you can't imitate what you've never seen.

Opportunities for acquiring social skills are absent from our society. If we had them once and know they're missing, we can figure out a way to provide them, again. If we want to see more marriages, we must introduce our young people to each other in wholesome situations, where they can get to know each other.

# Kicking the Recipe Across the Table
## Options for Living

1. Do you enjoy living with others?

2. Is your need for personal space greater than your need for companionship?

3. Have you ever lived alone? If you have, was it a fulfilling time?

4. Have you developed a satisfying social life around a small, select group of friends?

5. Do you find yourself predominately in the company of female friends?

6. When you think of the concept of "home," what does it look and feel like?

7. Are you working at making your perception of "home" a reality?

8. If you lived with a same-sex housemate, would you be concerned about the appearance of being a homosexual?

9. Would you live with a same-sex seasoned person for improved financial, emotional and spiritual support?

# Keeping the Presence of Men

It is the nature of men and women to want each other's company. According to the Christian Bible, God created woman because man was lonely. The relationship between Adam and Eve is well known, including their not so excellent apple adventure.

As Seasoned Women, we have learned that men do not define us, but we know the importance of men in our lives. They keep us anchored in our very different roles. Having men in our lives adds to the quality of life. Men add the spice that completes us.

Depending on what stage of life we're in, men appear as our co-stars in different real-life dramas. For instance, my first memory of what being male meant to me was my mom and dad telling me to leave my older brother alone, and play with my sister.

Joseph had the private bedroom. He had his private things and friends who crowded in to talk about things that my sister and I were not permitted to hear. We had to stay away from the boys. As males, their space was respected.

I was always with my sister, Paulette. We were close in every sense of the word. We were female and on the second floor of our family flat, our twin beds were side by side. We slept in a bedroom filled with ruffles.

Through our window, we could look directly into Ada Lee's bedroom, in the building next door. The red brick buildings were close enough for us to talk back and forth.

The other girls on the block were a part of our play routine, but the boys operated without us. We could see each other, in those days, as we went about doing whatever we did around the block. Though we were separated, I enjoyed the distance from the boys.

As a small child, I remember sitting in the laps of women, not men. When they'd give me summer hugs, the smell of powder or cornstarch on their bosoms gave off wonderful fragrances that are forever embedded in my memory. The women's exquisite scents were mixed with perspiration, as their loving arms squeezed the breath out of my small frame.

Sometimes, I'd get a whiff of Evening in Paris perfume that came from a shapely royal blue bottle. In the spring, my mother used Dorothy Gray, a fragrance that smelled of delicate lilacs. It was a pleasant scent, but it was called, of all things, toilet water. It could never match the mysterious scent in the royal blue bottle on the glass tray of my mother's vanity.

In those St. Louis days, Evening in Paris perfume was the rage. I couldn't wait to dab some behind my ears. As with most curious girls, I wanted to see if what I imagined would happen actually happened. See, I imagined by applying Evening in Paris, I could feel what Paris was all about.

When we were near the men in the family, the manner in which we received hugs was different and we never sat in their laps. My mother's understanding of human nature made her train Paulette and me to politely discourage or receive male hugs from a distance.

During that innocent stage of our lives, males were always around, but we girls were taught to adhere to a guideline that kept some space between them and us.

The first time I was allowed to talk about a boy liking me — whatever that meant — was when I started school. Even though I knew what the words meant, the concept was strange, at first because the boy that turned out liking me was the one I reported to the teacher for hitting me.

Assuring me that the boy wasn't being mean, the wiser, older girls in the schoolyard told me that it was really that he liked me. That began my neophyte realization that there were things that happened between some boys and girls that didn't happen between others in the same group.

I also learned that my father reacted more harshly than my mother to the idea of my having a little boyfriend. This amazed me because even though my mother was always the cautious one of my parents, she was the one who thought it was cute to have a little girl popular with the boys.

However, when my menstrual cycle started at 13 and my hormones kicked in full blast, mom no longer thought it was cute. Having a popular big girl gave her little pleasure.

She encouraged me to develop friendships with boys and nothing more. By then, my body was singing a whole different song. I was beginning to enjoy boys more than I thought possible. I wondered how I could have been so wrong in my thinking. This boy thing wasn't such a bad idea, after all. I was amazed by how much they had changed.

To keep parental control over our activities, my mom and dad made our household clubhouse central. The Thomas Street flat we lived in welcomed boys as a natural part of the social scene. It was there that I developed social skills with males. The home was an excellent training ground to find out what attracted the attention of boys.

I was able to observe male and female interaction within the safety of our home.

As little girls, we learned about female and male roles in the community. My adult responses to life were shaped by childhood experiences. By the time I was 18 years old, I knew how men responded to me.

Most of a female's initial male relationships come from the pool of boys they know from school and the neighborhood. Except for a few trips and summers away from home, experiences outside the community are limited. Most first loves and sex partners come from school or the community.

## The Company of Men

I enjoy being in the company of men even more as I have grown older. Aging hasn't dimmed my expectations. I have not suffered abuse from men. A female's positive relationships with men don't happen by accident. They come as a result of how she is groomed.

Currently, dysfunctional relationships between the sexes are expected. All I can say is that for over forty years, my expectations of having positive relationships with men have been met. Few things happen by accident. My peers that showed up to eat chili and franks, play bid whist, dance and sing Doo-Wop were where they needed to be to learn how to function in each other's company. It wouldn't have worked without being among role models to respect.

My life hasn't changed much. I still have many wonderful mostly single men who are at my apartment for reasons usually associated with food. We go out dancing, dining or walking the streets, together. I'm not intimate with them, but they give me a wonderful feeling of being a woman.

I'm old school when it comes to men. I make it clear to them how I see my role as a woman. I don't confuse a man. He already has too much mystery about a woman to solve.

Having no fear of domestic life, I love to cook for my man, and our friends and family. Since I'm comfortable with myself, I'm happy in almost any situation. So far, that has been an attractive thing to men.

I try to remain open for the changes that surely will come. I'm old enough to feel secure in what I do, but young enough for spontaneity. I like being me with a man. No matter how great an actress you are, no one can wear a mask forever. And who, in their right mind, would want to?

In spite of sounding like an echo of the Golden rule, if I have learned anything about what succeeds with a man, it is that you treat him like you want him to treat you.

It's like raising a plant. You place it in the best soil, with the appropriate light exposure and then water as needed. Too much sun and water and the plant will die. Rough handling will make the leaves fall off.

However, when you pay attention and talk to plants, they'll let you know when it's time for a change. A plant's beauty and growth are unpredictable and dependent on others.

Sometimes, your man is your gardener. He is capable of cultivating your beauty, provided you supply the rich soil. Men's feelings aren't as different from women's as their behavior suggests.

From the perspective of two decades, I have gained some insights into men. When dealing with platonic or romantic relationships, this Seasoned Woman has some advice to share.

# Nothing Ventured, Nothing's Gained

***Do not look for a man, if you're lonely.*** They seem to have radar and hide. They know the signs of hunting women. They run away from well-dressed groups of three or four women who come early and stay late. Do not be the hunter.

***Going out with a poplar platonic male friend is the ultimate way to meet men.*** It gives you a chance to sit back and observe them. Think of it as an open audition they don't know they're giving.

Spend time shopping and running errands with your male pal. Have drinks and dinner at his favorite watering hole. Joining him at his friend's place to watch sports is effective. Small groups of men get together to watch sports, all the time. However, be sure you know the sport well. If you don't, your cover could be blown.

***While in their company, pay close attention to their conversation.*** You'll discover who they are by what they say and do. Also, by the way they respond to each other, you'll figure out each man's status in the group and his true disposition.

The man who, on the surface, seems to be Mr. Wonderful can, while reacting with friends, show shallowness, a temper or a tendency to be overly critical. What you're looking for is a man who in acting without the mask he may wear otherwise.

Also, especially with a new woman present, men naturally, even unconsciously exhibit a display of macho one-upsmanship when interacting with each other. You can make mental notes about someone who interests you, for future reference.

If there are men interested, you will know from your friend, either before you leave or later. Both married and unmarried men may want to give you some play. While it's your decision, it's extremely bad form to use your friend to hook up with a married man or one who doesn't express an interest in you to your friend.

It's been a topic of discussion over the years that favorable sexual attraction is spontaneous. But many women respond to a certain type of man. Likewise, I'm convinced that men have a female type that they prefer over others. Men are resourceful when they see a woman they want. With or without the help of your male friend, he will find a way to contact you. Resume your normal routine. Once you have made yourself accessible, you don't have to continue putting yourself in his path.

I remember when a man was trying to contact me. He was the essence of the male hunter. At different times of the day, he would cruise my block, trying to happen upon me because he didn't know my exact address. When I allowed him to "accidentally" run into me, he wouldn't let me go until I gave him some contact information.

***Do not re-arrange your life to fit his schedule.*** Men will voluntarily re-arrange their lives to spend more time with you. It's unnecessary to press him to be with you. He'll be around as much as it takes for those white-hot emotions of an early romance to cool to two-digit Fahrenheit.

In the early stages, you may discover that you see more of him than your time allows. His constant presence is establishing unspoken territorial rights. Because of the shared chemistry, few women are able to resist the intoxicating feeling of being the object of his familiarizing affection.

***Men will call you when they miss you.*** Although they deny it, men like to know where you are. I don't buy into the female rules that advise a woman to never be too available. Always return his calls promptly and don't play games, pretending to be busy or out when the phone rings.

In the beginning, you should call sparingly until you get a feel for the rhythm of his telephone habits. Until then, be a conservative caller, but understand that most men love talking on the phone as much as women. They don't approach a phone call as a bargain basement therapy session. For them, a phone call is no different from hanging out on the corner or meeting at a bar to plan the evening.

Simultaneously to talking to women on the phone, men often watch television, eat snacks and drink. As a result, you may discover he gets distracted much easier than you. A phone conversation isn't the way most men prefer to work on specific relationship issues, so be prepared to repeat some points when you see him in person.

It is well established that a woman's verbal ability is superior to that of a man. When you discuss an area of conflict between you and your man, don't take it personally if you have to repeat your complaint more than once. Frequently, men don't remember specific details of what you've discussed with them.

***Men have impeccable "selective" memory.*** They easily remember and do what's important for them. Men almost never forget anything that pertains to them. In the news recently, there was a story reported about a man who absentmindedly left his sleeping son in his car, with fatal results.

Thankfully, this is rare. However, a man can remember events, dates and people with amazing accuracy if they're an important part of his world.

Women learn early to consider other people and to be thoughtful in their dealings with them. In relationships with men, we're usually the ones who remember special occasions such as anniversaries. Women remember things and incorporate the recognition of them into a relationship, which keeps it moving smoothly.

Mothers are responsible for passing on recipes that include a large measure of consideration for others. It's a good recipe that can turn out bad, if we aren't careful. You can be left with a hollow feeling, if your man doesn't at least try to remember things you deem important.

A woman can either be forever hurt by a man repeatedly forgetting important things or she can understand that men were brought up differently than we were. Provide subtle reminders. Remember, he's gotten older, too, and his seasoned mind needs a little help from time to time.

While men forget important things, they expect a woman to remember. If you do forget his birthday or anything pertaining to him, it can create quite an angry reaction. Men are easily hurt, if they are overlooked.

If you concentrate on what you enjoy, his forgetting won't hurt your feelings — not much, anyway. Anyway, don't nag him. Let his conscience nag him into buying you a great gift or giving you a surprise night out.

**Have a life.** Do things that are independent of his life. This is especially important to keep the attention of men who are over 50. They have adopted a particular lifestyle for a half century or more and are comfortable with it.

When you get involved with a man, you may not be his only sex partner. If he decides to become your lover exclusively, he will. It's not your call. The best that you can do is maintain what it was about you that attracted him in the first place. Many women lose themselves trying to be someone they thought a man wanted.

***Do not invite yourself out with him, if he does not offer to invite you first.*** Not only is it bad manners, it could be an encroachment from which you can never recover. Let him invite you out. Being too aggressive can scare a man away.

Neither of you wants to feel tied to the other. You should only put him on your social calendar if the situation is convenient for both of you. Eventually, you will create a routine that works.

You both will know where you want to go with each other and where you don't. I encourage my man to do things without me. It shows him that I trust him. It also lets him know the girl can do things for herself.

***Men expect and respond positively to praise, just as you do.*** For the great and small things a man does for you, express your appreciation. Be far more generous with compliments than complaints and treat compliments like money that you generously give and graciously receive. As far as criticism goes, I suggest that you consider it a bill no one enjoys receiving.

As with death and taxes, criticism is inevitable. However, if you must criticize him, do so constructively, with the sensitivity you would hope for. Make it a rule to criticize his behavior not him personally. Unless absolutely necessary, keep your critic's license in a drawer. Tell yourself that if no positive outcome results from your critical analysis, that it will stop.

That most men do not handle criticism well is no surprise to women. Since men are threatened by and get excited about the smallest, most ordinary situations, such as accepting help. Giving them directions when they appear to be lost, while driving to a destination is a smoking gun. The sensitivity I've gained over time allows me to enjoy the ride as the main event rather than quell ther volcanic response. Enjoy the time with him.

I pay close attention to details that are time-consuming and thoughtful, as opposed to expensive and grand. Without being asked, a man will find just the right size hinge to repair your cosmetic case, if he feels you appreciate what he does.

***It's called none of your business.*** Men will tell you what they want you to know. They want to keep a special part of themselves private (just like you). With very little conversation, most men will express likes and dislikes.

A man's need for privacy is demonstrated early in life. His boyhood treehouse was a place to be away from the scrutiny of the dreaded — at that age — girls that he enjoyed from a distance. As a grown man, the treehouse becomes cigar bars and private clubs.

Women have few exclusive domains about which men protest or go to court to become members. Women try to invade male treehouses from an early age and it continues throughout life. Almost never is the attempted invasion the other way around.

Today, women punch each other in the face and body to be called boxers. Some things aren't good for men or women. No matter what, women want to be "all up" in men's stuff.

Seasoned men have years of male-only activity. Let them have their fun. If you absolutely must be a part of their love of sports, let's say, learn the rules.

You don't have to share his passions, but it opens the door to communicating as an interested partner. Share the time as friends and don't view the activity as an enemy to your relationship.

Although my man loves boxing, I think it should be outlawed. Still, I make food for him and his guests. With my reading material, I sit on the floor and look in on them between rounds. We have a great time. They yell and cuss and laugh and eat. It's how they enjoy the event and each other's company.

Either you can accept a man's ideas of fun or make yourself miserable trying to change him. A measure of how much a woman loves a man is how much she allows him to enjoy things that give him pleasure.

Unless it's unreasonable, let him have his way, particularly if it involves something that doesn't impact you negatively and fulfills a need in him. It's been my experience that most men don't have too many unreasonable demands.

## Be an Informed Participant

The issue, at this point in our lives, is that we too have become selfish and unaccustomed to pleasing anyone except ourselves. We find it difficult to open our narrow thinking, but the quality of a relationship will be determined by our eagerness to accommodate the desires of another, while satisfying our own.

Establishing a friendship at the beginning of the relationship helps clarify many things before you become emotionally attached to a man. Getting to know him through other peoples' opinions of him is important, also. Investigate all the men you find interesting enough to know, especially seasoned men.

Even though women know some young men are dogs, they'd be wise to remember that an old dog is still dangerous. Some men have a long history of mistreating women. Not all pimps are young men. Check him out before you leap into the unknown.

If you meet a man that none of your associates know, it's possible to luck out and find a winner. However, be careful. You be the one to investigate the best bank for your money or the best place to vacation. You choose the locks for your residence and schools for your children.

Don't be shy about checking out the person you're thinking of trusting with your heart. When there are so many sources of information to tap into these days, it makes sense to discover as much about a man as you can.

Whenever you hear a man say "take my word" for something or "trust me," a blowing-smoke alarm should go off on the ceiling of your brain. He may be telling the truth, but until you're sure of him, continue to ask him questions, such as the names of places, friends and incidents.

What you're listening for are inconsistencies. Even a good liar trips up, every now and then. And it's always possible you'll hear the name of someone you know while he's spelling out his network of friends and acquaintances.

If he mentions someone you know, you'll have someone to give you the 411 on him. Avoid an obvious inquisition, but gather information during the course of a casual conversation. As some extremists have done, don't go through his garbage, his unattended wallet, stored phone numbers or follow him around like a private detective. If you're that suspicious, walk away or see him casually.

Another way to determine a man's character is to observe how he treats his mother and sister. It will tell you a lot about his attitude toward women. Their relationship will tell you about his sense of responsibility and generosity.

# Practice Objective Listening

If you are a careful listener, he will tell you everything that you need to know. The trick to gaining valuable information is to accept what he says without hearing what you hope he is saying. When you want only that man, listening may become dangerously selective.

If things are moving too quickly and you don't feel comfortable, slow down to a speed you can navigate. Then, if your gut feeling continues to say no, don't do it.

Sometimes when the stars are perfectly aligned, everything comes together in a relationship. Oh, there may be some rough corners that have to be smoothed, but if there's anything like real-life magic, romance is where you find it.

Conversely, when the stars are not only misaligned, but keep crashing into each other, you will know that, too. Your inner lack of ease may be indicated by the flashing yellow light that says, "stop on red."

Remember, communication happens through your five senses of hearing, sight, touch, smell and taste. Don't forget the sixth sense — instinct. Nature's gift of instinct is the most basic sense that we have.

Instinct is not scientifically quantifiable, but it should never be ignored. Unexplained, troubling vibes about a man who could become a serious lover should be thoroughly examined before deciding the viability of a relationship.

While waiting for your instinct to be confirmed by opportunity and time, ask yourself if you really want this man to be Mr. Right.

As a Seasoned Woman, the time lost in a bad relationship is precious. Bouncing back gets even harder.

# Getting the Lumps Out of the Gravy

While the combustible chemistry between you in the early stages of romance is a threat to world security, talk as much as possible. If you're creative, getting to know him can become a really fun adventure.

It may be some time since your last love affair. If so, you need to approach it with a flexibility that may be new to you. It's not so much desperation, as the mentally challenged might conclude, as it is your realization that things you'd never compromise about as a young woman somehow seem less important.

And at this wisdom stage, you might even wonder why things you fought to keep in relationships when you were young ever really mattered. A blessing is that at this age, the really important stuff is easier to separate from what doesn't matter.

Remember, you're bringing an already full lifetime into the picture. Therefore, it's crucial for you to begin with a style that is easy to maintain because it's honest.

Be enthusiastic about your new man, but keep your needs and limitations in mind, as well as his. Neither one of you is in the springtime of life. So don't lose yourself in infatuation. This time together gives you a chance to communicate your expectations of each other.

Set up an environment that encourages conversation. Initially, men visit our space for dinner, drinks and eventually sex. Since we are usually the host, we should set the tempo and mood: turn off the television, lower the lights and the music. Then, slip into something so comfortable for you that it's uncomfortable for him.

Always control the quality of shared time as much as possible. Keep the intimacy by turning off cell phones and the volume on your answering machine.

It is impossible to regain the intense feelings of anticipation and excitement that a man and woman experience before being intimate that first time. Since it is to be cherished, take your time. As Otis Redding once sang, "While you're there waiting, just anticipating, try just a little tenderness."

The pre-sex stage can be used productively to determine how you want your relationship to go. As is usually the case, a woman has a distinct advantage over the man. When an aroused man is forced to delay gratification, he is more agreeable to a woman's ground rules than he might normally be.

You have his total attention and he wants to be cooperative. Now is the time to get the condom. He won't like it, but as sensuously as possible, help him put it on. Be creative in safely getting what you want, the way you want it. This is how you set the stage for him keeping you special.

## Taste Before Serving

A new man in your bed is always like the first time, all over again. The drama is intense because of the expectations of fulfillment. Choose the time well, so that neither of you have to get up right away. Make sure you have plenty of lay-around talk time and an opportunity to have sex again, if he's up to it.

Most of all, sex should not happen in a rush. But frantic sex can be fun, too. Many wonderful dishes are found on the lovemaking menu. And, oh, the favorite dessert women love so: holding onto each other afterward, whispering and slowly kissing. The rhythm slows down and loving caresses fade into blissful sleep.

Age has taught us the subtleties of precious, intimate moments. These can be savored while recalling the passion for and potential of a new love in the making. We learned patience to form a mature love.

It is important to tell him how you feel. If having sex with him was exciting, tell him what turned you on. Men want to be told they are powerful lovers. For some reason, a woman automatically assumes that she satisfied a man if he has an erection and ejaculates. Don't assume anything. Listen to what he says, after he awakens.

If you were not satisfied and did not reach a climax, pick your time carefully, but tell him. Since you're not a novice, tell him what might work better for you. The main thing is to pick the right time, so that it doesn't seem like criticism, instead of a suggestion aimed at making it better.

Men have paper-thin egos when it comes to their sexual potency or lack their of. It seems that the older they get, the more anxious they get about it. Impotence causes them great concern because erections are difficult to get and maintain.

The thing about men of all ages that never changes is that, after sex, they immediately go to sleep.

## Intimacy is Golden

As time passes, lovemaking can become more fulfilling. I have found that the emotional ties, strengthened by shared experiences, add flavor to the sex act. Daily events are spice in the lovemaking pot, waiting to be heated up.

Lovemaking is never finished. It is always a work in progress. The closeness that binds you and gives you a feeling of unity can often reduce you to tears, in each other's arms.

Relationships require more work as they evolve from the infatuation stage to the engagement stage. When the passion of the new sex ebbs, the strength of your bond is tested. If you lean on each other in difficult times, the chances are greater that your love will survive.

If statistics hold true, each of you has a full life, complicated by aging parents, adult children, grandchildren, sickness and dying, and increasing health problems of your own. Coping with these situations as a couple can serve to bring you closer than ever.

It would take a psychopath not to embrace another human being who has provided dependable support during the hard times. Sometimes, moments of the greatest love come when a person remembers the one who was always there to lend encouragement or a shoulder to cry on, or just was someone to listen when you talked out loud about life so it didn't spirit you away.

Quiet talks in the middle of the night or refrigerator raids after a late night out, or sitting on the beach holding hands while watching the surf roll in and out sends nonverbal messages between two people. Sometimes, eye contact alone is enough to keep fueling the passion.

My most vivid memory of intimacy is burned into my heart. Paulette, my mother and I had just had a snack in the cafeteria of the hospital where my father was having a respiration therapy session. We went back to the room at the end of the session. There we were met with the news that only forty-five minutes after we left him, daddy had died.

Daddy was lying there with the sports page of the newspaper and his glasses nearby. His mouth was slightly open. Mother slipped away from us and went to him. She had such a loving spirit that it pierced the stillness of the room. She gently placed her hand on his face so softly that he wouldn't have wakened, even if he only slept.

Mother's palm circled daddy's face and smoothed his eyebrows, then stopped on his lips. She closed the small open space at the center of his mouth and straightened his head on the pillow. She said, "Oh baby, I'm so sorry I wasn't here."

It was the intimacy of a lifetime. There was no room for anyone else in my mother's last expression of love for my daddy. My sister and I were their children, but these two Vashon High School sweethearts who married, survived the Great Depression and lived to enjoy lives full of healthy children, grandchildren and great-grandchildren said goodbye, alone.

## I Want a Lover Not Just a Friend

Having a male friend that's like a brother is only wonderful if neither party has a serious interest in the other. If you're a woman harboring feelings for a friend because your circumstances or his prevented you from speaking up, or you never found the courage to speak up, you should show him what he's missing.

Transform yourself into his greatest female fantasy. You, above all people, have access to his inner-most thoughts. You know him because he tells you his secrets.

The friendship role is comfortable and convenient. Unfortunately, many women stay in it because they are afraid to approach a man they care about. Of course, there are men you're close to and a romance would make a friendship impossible.

Leave that kind of relationship alone. If you're sure he has no romantic interest in you, don't take the chance.

However, if you're always the one sitting in the back seat being dropped off at home first or find yourself sitting across from him at the table, shake things up, if you don't like it. You could invent a reason to be taken home last. This will allow you to end up alone with him. I don't have to tell you this opens up possibilities your feverish mind has been contemplating for quite a while. Your tone of voice should make it clear to him that you are definitely not his sister.

Having a nightcap or an early breakfast together could be just the setting to bury your brother/sister relationship and replace it with something less incestuous. If you're like most women, much of your time has been spent doing favors for him. You both can be so used to that, it's become a habit.

It's an unfortunate fact of life that as single men get older, they usually require more assisted living to cover their domestic and social needs. Many never learned to cook or shop for themselves or — unbelievably — never selected a comprehensive primary care doctor or a dentist.

As a close friend, you may find yourself acting as his personal assistant in helping him with domestic chores such as doing laundry or running errands.

Although he is not technically your man, he gets a lot of your time. Your relationship has endured for a reason. If it's a good relationship, it's probably one that has benefited you both.

If knowing that all of this might be lost if you tell him of your desire for a romance you are still intent on taking the chance, be prepared to live with the results.

If your choice is full speed ahead, I suggest you tell him that you are tired of being alone and want to meet someone. In the course of saying this, be sure to let him know, in no uncertain terms, that you want him to stop looking at you as his sister. While you might be close friends with a man, he can't read your mind. Tell him what you want.

It's unfortunate, but true, that most men aren't sensitive enough to pick up on anybody's loneliness except their own. It's possible that he'll pick up on the clues you give him that you're hungry for his deeper attention. If he does appreciate your feelings, but isn't interested, try not to change your ideas about his character.

If he says no thanks and makes an effort to hook you up with his friends, don't react with hurt. He's probably doing it because he cares, not because he wants to end your friendship.

## Enjoy the Fun, Friend

There is a mature womanly art to working the room while on the arm of a friend. Since no one knows that he's just your friend, it's another good situation to meet men. You are guaranteed a dance partner and a feeling of security. You are free to meet and flirt with his friends or anyone you like upon first meeting. For any Seasoned Woman, it's a perfectly delightful paradox, this being free, but taken.

Don't forget to act like his date and not his sister. Old habits are tougher to break than you know. Don't take lint off his jacket, straighten his tie or fuss over him like his mother, either. You're out to enjoy an evening of endless flirtation.

Dress as alluringly as you would on a romantic date. Spend money and time on a dress that shows off your legs or any other outstanding part of your body. If your hips, thighs and waistline are shapely, you can wear slacks with a daringly skimpy top.

However, stay away from a long jacket pant suit that looks like you're trying to hide. So you can walk gracefully, always wear sexy shoes that are comfortable.

When going out with a purpose, never — I repeat, never — wear new shoes. Wear them at home and around the neighborhood for a while before you go out. There's nothing less attractive than body language that reflects hurting feet.

Keep your jewelry, makeup and hair simple, but elegant. Remember, it's important to get some sleep before you go out. You don't want a man coming up to you and after looking at your eyes, asking, "May I take your bags?"

Each woman has her own social clock that tells her when to arrive for the greatest impact, but I'd say the best time to make an entrance is when the scene is filled with energized people. Riding that wave, you become the fresh, new face.

As you wait for your "date" to return from checking your coats, you can make eye contact with any man that's in your chemistry class. And why not look? You are available, just not so easily claimed.

Oh, the men can look and even speak to you, but not get too close. After all, you have a date, for as long as no one interests you.

A woman knows that part of peaking a man's interest requires that she surround herself with an air of mystery. Make him want to discover who you are.

If asked for your phone number, make it a point to never write it on a piece of paper. (Thank God our generation can, both, show some class and keep it real.) Accept his business card or give him yours, if you're interested.

Take a few solo walks around the venue to give other men a chance to see you. Allow them to engage you in brief conversation. Early in the evening, carry and drink juice or water from a stemmed glass. This keeps your brain clear, and your eyes and face will look fresher longer. Don't have alcoholic drinks until just before you're ready to leave.

Don't be afraid to initiate light conversation with men. Comments about the music, the food and the people in attendance are good topics. Engaging in polite conversation with strange men won't damage your pristine reputation. Anyway, after the brief interludes, you'll return to your friend. It is with him that you should have the first dance and the last.

By the end of the evening, your friend will probably ask you out again on a fun date. If he chooses not to romance you along with it, he can still be helpful by safely exposing you to other potential lovers.

A man may look at your friend and wish he were him. Later, he may discover he can be your friend and your lover, just not your brother.

## If All Else Fails, Go for It Solo

Maybe you don't want the company of a male friend. Sometimes, you may just want to go out alone. Clubs are OK, but private parties are better. A single Seasoned Woman should navigate a house party differently than a club. Make a statement by dressing in a unique way. This is the time to pull out the really interesting pieces of jewelry: the one-of-a-kind necklace, the exotic earrings and bracelet, and the strange ring that all spark conversation.

Don't wear black unless it highlights a fabulous part of your body. Black is overrepresented and easily forgotten unless it stands out in a man's mind.

Don't have a large handbag or wear sunglasses and sit in the same place all night talking to other women. Be a mysterious diva for a few hours. Float around.

Be sure not to take food or fixings. Be prepared to do nothing beyond handing the host a bottle of wine or flowers, as you enter. Do not get there toward the end of the evening, when the party is breaking up. You want to be able to move about, freely socializing and spending time talking in different groups.

Circulate and introduce yourself to circles of strangers. If you're a bit shy, position yourself next to a friendly social extrovert. The extrovert likes the feeling of pulling everybody into their own personal party called life. They enjoy the power of knowing everybody, especially exotic women. Let them help make your night.

Never station yourself near the entrance or the bathroom area. You'll be greeted frequently, but only other women will engage you in conversation. Women always line up and hover around the bathroom, while men tend to quickly enter and exit the facility.

Periodically chill by standing near a window or repairing to the room where the TV is. Leave with the second wave of guests. Staying too long gives the impression that you're waiting to be approached.

If a man shows interest in you, he can always ask the host of the party about that mysterious creature he simply has to see, again. Then, the host can let you know about the man's desire to contact you.

Also, you can take the initiative to inquire about someone you've seen. Don't call him, however. Through the party host, find out where the man hangs out and arrange to go there accompanied by the host. Do this once. If he shows interest and acts on it, then you made a discreet move that paid off.

The unfortunate reality is that the pool of healthy men quickly diminishes once we pass age 45, but don't let that conjure up a celibate future for you, living in a convent with just a memory of male companionship. The bottom line is that you must imagine a man in your life before he becomes a reality.

As to Seasoned Women of a different stripe, there is a considerable number of them who don't care whether they spark the interest of a man or not. They don't have to be gay to feel this way. Apparently, it is what they need and feel for now.

While some of these women will become active in the romance game later on, others will not. And that, too, is fine. No one thing satisfies us all. I respect all Seasoned Women and all their desires.

# Kicking the Recipe Across the Table
## Keeping the Presence of Men

1. Do you get a special feeling in the company of men that's important to you, no matter how old you get? Explain your response.

2. How important is it to have a husband in your life?

3. Can a woman be perceived as masculine because of the role she plays?

4. Is same-sex partnering a viable lifestyle for aging women?

5. What satisfactions come from living without a man?

6. Can a platonic relationship be a rich and meaningful one?

7. Is a male presence the same as a male present?

8. What is male presence in your life and how has it changed from when you were young?

# Being the Seasoned "Other" Woman

The other woman is referred to in many ways: the honey on the side, the girlfriend and the mistress are a few names that can be printed. She is more than a cultural cliche. The "other" woman grows older like everybody else. When reality sets in and she sadly realizes that her entire life has been wasted, living on the hope that her married man will one day make her number one, it is not a pretty picture.

Her married or otherwise committed man will not be there when her children by him go to bed or wake up, every day. He won't help them with their homework or see them off to school. Her unequally divided man will not carve the Thanksgiving turkey or ring in the New Year with her. He'll be home with his wife and legitimate children. This bitter pill is a tough reality for the aging "other" woman to swallow.

These Seasoned Other Women that are emotionally tied to these men face a life even more dire than the rest of the aging population. Few thought they would be in such a relationship, forever. They looked up and suddenly, they weren't 30 or 35, anymore. Being the 50-year-old other woman wasn't anybody's plan. But what do they do?

The other women that candidly spoke to me tried to put a happy face on their lives. In what I perceived to be a case of sour grapes, many of them ridiculed the institution of marriage.

Some even stated that their quality of life was superior to married women because, as single women involved with married men, they were spared the stress of the legal wife. Interestingly, none of these women preferred having their children raised in a single-mother household. All wanted full-time fathers for their children, but accepted a part-time mate.

While many of the other women had more than one child by the same married man, a surprising number had children by different married men. Even if it wasn't their plan, there did seem to be a pattern of poor judgment. Neither race, education nor economic level made a difference in their choices.

It would be a miracle if youth ever foresaw or planned to be middle-aged. Most of us arrive at 50 less prepared than we would like to be. Preparation is usually viewed in terms of financial security and fine health. However, as women, we must early on consider the far-reaching implications of misplaced love and loyalty.

Allowing a man into your heart is different from allowing one into your bed. Planning takes the time and patience for which youth has no time. And as we all know, young love is a sand dial with an endless amount of sand.

Young and old men have one thing in common. They expect distinctly different things from different women. Based on what women bring into their lives, men select and separate. They know which woman to take where and which one to treat as though she's special. They are unflinchingly honest about ranking their women.

Whether they admit it or not, men have a mental picture of the type of woman they would choose for a wife to be the mother of their children. The quality of the sex may be important to a man in his choice of woman, but it isn't the most important factor when selecting a life partner.

A harsh reality is that a large percentage of people today are the result of unwanted pregnancies. Without planning for it, young men and women are forced into unwanted relationships only because they produced a child. Whether they try to make the best of a bad situation, find unexpected love in the course of doing the honorable thing or never see each other again in life, their actions of youth will affect their seasoned years well beyond 50.

As a group, young and older men seldom raise the children from unwanted pregnancies. Even if they send money for child support, most men still marry the woman they want to marry and not the one that fathering a child forces on them.

My research found that when women had babies very young (some as early as 14 years old), they often didn't get married to other men and remained sexually available to the father of their children. Frequently, these young women take on the role of the "other" woman as teenagers and remain entrapped for the rest of their lives.

When it comes to how Seasoned Men respond to unwanted pregnancies as compared to their young, male counterparts, my personal survey of over two hundred men suggests that age does not matter. Seasoned men, like younger men, sometimes financially support the mothers, but don't necessarily marry them, particularly since many of them are already married.

I should add that those men who are not forthcoming with money to support their children have been forced by state law to pay child support. If they fail to do so and leave the area to escape paying, they are tracked down by law enforcement.

# The Road to Number Two

If you pay attention, the behavior of the man you call "your man" tells you your rank, immediately. Ask yourself these questions: When does he see me? What time does he visit? Where does he take me? What does he call me when he introduces me — my honey, my girl, my lady or does he only use my name? To whom does he introduce me?

Certain signs a woman sometimes ignores can tell her all she needs to know about whether a man intends to commit to a relationship or not. If you're going to be groomed to be woman number two, at least confront him on it. If you don't challenge his maneuvering, he'll only try to get away with more audacious behavior. You have to let him know you're not a fool and that you have respect for yourself. If you don't, he sure won't.

After good sex or the thrill of falling in love, many women lose the ability to read a man. They don't really hear what a man is saying between the lines. These failures have caused a lot of women to fall into the category forever known as the other woman.

The course of the life of a woman on the way to becoming the other woman is always a straight path that can be charted. Some fight the position they find themselves falling into, while others yield to something stronger than they. Their daily lives go on and, at some point, reaches a plateau disguised as what's normal.

If the relationship lasts a few years, the man, the other woman and the wife accept the triangle. If the wife finds out what's going on and decides to get a divorce, it usually happens early. Otherwise, it becomes a routine where the wife has the control. Only she can rock his world: economics, community image, professional image, his status with the children and other family members. Her decision to remain or walk with civility has direct consequences for the Seasoned Older Other Woman.

When the other woman begins to panic about her unchangeable situation as she ages, she uses every means possible to pressure the man into leaving his wife. Maybe she never said so, but all these years, the other woman has envied the wife's position. Down deep, she is furious and hurt that he does not love her enough to leave home and marry her. Also, she may be frightened that once the spice of the forbidden wears off, she can be dumped by him or, just as bad, be discarded if the wife demands it.

By the time she's 40, the other woman feels the pressure to take a stand and do something daring. Age is forcing her hand, especially if she hasn't had children. For her to be childless and unmarried is what usually sets her off.

In their 40s, many of these women choose to have babies by men who are not free to marry them. Some give up on the prospect of the man divorcing his wife. They decide to become a single parent rather than never parent a child at all.

Statistics show that the number of women who raise children without husbands has increased tremendously over the last thirty years.

The United States Census Report of 1998 states that:
- About 21 percent of never-married women have given birth to at least one child
- Between 1970 and 1996, the number of single parents increased from 3.8 million to 11.7 million
- Approximately 19.8 million children under age 18 live with only one parent. About 84 percent of them live with mothers who have never married

Seasoned Women who have the married man's children don't have the advantages the wife enjoys. In the shadow of the man's primary home, the aging other woman fulfills both his and her family obligations, alone. It is usually her mother and family that help her raise his children.

Statistics from the Census further show that in 1997, there were 266,490,000 people in the United States. Of that number, approximately 37,000,000 lived below the poverty level. Among families maintained by women with no husband present, 32.4 percent were poor.

Pre-schoolers in poor families were 50 percent more likely to be cared for by their grandparents and other relatives than those of non-poor families (36% versus 24%). About 4 million children live in the household of their grandparents, representing 5.6 of all the children under age 18.

By age 50, the other woman knows that whatever benefits she received in her younger years will represent her package. When her seasoned married man retires, she knows that a slower phase of their relationship begins. She has accepted his wife as a permanent fixture, just as the wife has tolerated her.

She is also clear that he will neither provide for her in his will nor place her name on any of his property, assets or bank accounts.

He may have given her a few credit cards over the years. However, her so-called man rarely makes meaningful arrangements for her. This is especially galling for a woman who has devoted her life to someone else's man.

As dispassionate as I tried to be when interviewing some of these women, I was nonetheless affected by the amazing stories of faithfulness that I heard. Some women reported being 100%

faithful to a man who was 100% married to another woman. As they say, you do the math.

It appears that other women are born, not made. The other woman's mentality for acceptance begins as youths, when failing to look at the big picture is epidemic.

Many young girls start out as other-women-in-training, a role they see as a power position, when pitted against a man's woman or wife. Her ego is puffed up by the thought that she is satisfying some need in the man that only her incomparable sex can.

## Graduating from Trainee to Full-Blown Other Woman

The other woman thinks that her married man needs her because of the regularity of his irregular attention. She remains in close proximity to always be accessible, just in case he has time to come by. She makes sure he has a key to her door for whenever he wants to use it.

A door key is literal and symbolic. It gives the man unlimited access. His freedom of movement in and out of her home, on his terms, locks her in and discourages any other male competitor. By her actions, she agrees to man-sharing.

Rarely does the other woman escape a dramatic confrontation with the married man's wife. Because of her second-class status, the other woman is almost always the loser in such a meeting. If the wife appears to round up her wayward husband and drag him home, the wife is more empowered than ever before. He almost always leaves with her.

The other woman who tries to place herself next to the head of the table seldom gets invited back to dinner. If she is invited back, she eats in the kitchen. There is a humble posture that the other woman has to be willing to assume in public.

## Wake Up, You're Old Enough to Walk

The other woman can exert more control over the situation by setting some guidelines. If the man wants to keep you on hold, demand that he agree to some demands. If you can't negotiate a wedding ring or holiday visits, you can require that he makes you financially secure. As you age, this will become even more important.

After all, what can you do with a pile of 14k jewelry, a large-screen television or clothes? You can buy that for yourself. Think about your future. If he dies of a heart attack (which could well happen doing double duty), you won't be left high and dry at 65.

Don't be shy. Let him make all the payments on a large life insurance policy and enroll you in a stock plan. Legally, you don't qualify for any of his benefits, no matter how many years you have been together.

His wife, of course, will receive her share of his benefits. All you will be left is the memory of being there for him when she was not. Some married men need a freaky sex partner that the other woman provides. Often, this diversion enhances the sex with his wife.

Cheating men told me that they enjoy different music, certain foods and drug parties with their other woman. They couldn't indulge in these activities with their wives. It only works for them with the other woman. They confessed that there are areas of their lives reserved for only them and their mistresses.

There are thousands of Seasoned Other Women, unmarried, aging honeys on the side that sacrificed full, young lives for married men. From Japan to the Mississippi Delta, these women cruelly face life alone all over the world.

## Women Can Also Plan

The late Dr. Lovenger Bowden always said that a failure to plan is a plan to fail.

As we put the finishing touches on the meal of life, this recipe forces a Seasoned Other Woman to ask, "Who will be there with me?" Dining alone with only a television for company is never our first choice.

If you're content with part of a man, a sometimes man, you've bought into being the other woman. If you have, be sure to take care of yourself early in the relationship, so that you grow old with some security. Remember to accumulate real property: real estate, stocks, treasury bonds and a retirement plan. Make doubly sure that your name is only attached to things that are fully paid off by him.

An insured car, registered in your name but paid monthly by him, is a jolly gift at Christmas time. If men live shorter lives than we do, it's only right that they provide for us before leaving us behind.

No one knows what the future holds for the other woman. Therefore, it is sensible to be prepared for the short side of life, especially when so many women live longer than their married men.

# Kicking the Recipe Across the Table
## Being the Seasoned "Other" Woman

1. Do you have intimate relationships with other women's husbands?

2. Is the other woman the blame for family break ups?

3. Can the other woman benefit from an affair of many years?

4. Is loneliness inevitable for the aging other woman?

5. Is it realistic to expect a married man to leave his wife and children for the other woman?

6. How should the wife treat her husband and his long-term lover?

7. Considering the shrinking pool of men 50 and over, is man-sharing the way to keep Seasoned Women from being alone?

8. What options are left for single women, if married men remain faithful and the scarcity of single men increases?

March 1, 2003

Dear Theda,

Let me begin with an apology. I regret that I've not been in touch, before now. I was truly glad to learn about your new marriage to Bill. My prayers are with you both for much happiness and a great future.

I was looking forward to celebrating with you on September 29, 2002. Unfortunately, my mom, who was 92 years old at the time, suffered a stroke on September 20, 2002.

To say the least, things became more complicated and events demanding on my time and emotions. My mom seemed to do fairly well to spite the challenge of the stroke.

On December 21, 2002, three months following the stroke, she had a heart attack and expired. My mom and I were very close. I was fully committed to her well being. The entire family gave it our best.

I've enclosed an obituary for your information. I have not even spoken to Carl about her passing. There remains so much to do.

I am just recently trying to get back to a routine. The grieving process is coming along. The family is doing fairly well. I hope that we can catch up, real soon.

Love as always,
*Gail*

# Cracks in the Heart

It is hard trying to recover from a broken heart. Experiencing loss causes the pain associated with heartache. To lose a loved one leaves a heavy sadness that no one can fully understand except the one left to grieve.

One way advancing age is reinforced in your mind is when you realize that you are regularly attending funerals. You find yourself at so many memorials to celebrate the lives of people with whom you shared so much life. Your stories were their stories.

These people contributed key ingredients to your evolution to the point you are now. They represent your vivid past and a future that isn't promised. As for the present, since you realize it is all you really have, wisely, you cherish all the moments.

Although as a Seasoned Woman you go on, a giant hole is left in your spirit. The hurt in your heart is a dull, thudding ache, like a pneumatic drill repeatedly jabbing concrete.

## Adult Orphans

When a child's parents die, the orphan is either taken in by other family or is embraced by a support system put in place for just such a catastrophe. However, when you're over 50 and lose a parent, you are on your own.

It's as though society expects adults to hurt less than the young. You are expected to recover quickly. After a week or two, you must return to work. Even for Seasoned Women, the loss of a parent creates an emotional graveyard where nothing ever really gets buried, not for long.

For us, falling apart is not an option. That would inconvenience our personal and professional dependents. For people who think the child in us died years ago, our showing the sorrow and pain of abandonment is disconcerting. It focuses attention on the fragility of life and inescapable death.

There is something in some inner recess of our brain that never fully accepts our own death as inevitable, until the mother who gave us life loses her own. Our denial of our own mortality takes a beating with the death of one parent, but denial ends when we are orphaned by the death of the second parent.

A mother's death is devastating. The matriarch who holds the family together with her wisdom, strength and love is irreplaceable glue. And without the queen bee, we are just so many drones fighting a sense of aimlessness.

As a small child, I remember seeing my mother cry. It scared me. I felt unprotected and naked. At 33, she was too old to be crying, I thought. She was the one that kept me safe. To see her cry at her grandmother's funeral left me confused and closer to pain than I ever want to be, again.

As the years passed, deaths in the family came like falling dominoes. Shortly after great grandmother was laid to rest, my mother's father died and then her mother, all of her best friends and then her husband of fifty-eight years.

Later, her brother passed and then she lost her only son. When her last close childhood friend died, I watched her become less tearful. Her grief was so deep and her heartache so severe that even as we held her, no one wanted to go near her wounded spirit.

The pain was not helped by our hugs and the kisses on her cheek or the pressing of her hand in ours. My mother quietly and prayerfully pulled herself along one day at a time, and put other people and activities in the place of the empty spaces. She filled what empty voids she could and the ones she couldn't fill, she left to memory.

She accepts that she will shed some tears over absent loved ones for the rest of her life. She expects it because heartaches will always come. However, she refuses to let the pain paralyze her as she goes about the daily routines of her unpredictable life.

My mother is my model for using an effective recipe for the ultimate heartache — death. Outliving your peers and your family leaves wounds that don't heal. Whenever I have been devastated by the loss of someone close to me, I remember my mother saying that, "nothing lasts forever."

Thousands of Seasoned Women of my generation have elderly parents and other relatives who have developed an amazing ability to repair themselves from the loss of loved ones. They continue to live with a strength and dignity that is inspirational.

Not surprisingly, their golden years are preoccupied with the universal concerns of their age group, that being where and how to live out the rest of their lives.

The battle for many of our parents is to remain independent and free of the need for a caregiver for as long as possible. Unless we are nurses or doctors by profession, we have minimal experience as caregivers.

Necessity is what thrusts us in the position, as it has down through human history. New to being caregivers, we frequently let our elders make unwise decisions because we love them and have always deferred to them.

## Assuming the Parental Role for Our Elders

"All the world's a stage," Shakespeare said, "and we but actors playing a part." However unfamiliar and foreign the role, we must step up and realize that in time, nature reverses the roles of parent and child. You become the parent and your parent the child. Depending on their mental state at an advanced age or because of a mental incapacity such as Alzheimer's or some other debility, their decision-making ability is diminished.

It is crucial to assist them in deciding on residency, health care and financial matters. This was brought home to me when I watched my nearly 80-year-old cousin Etta fall apart after the sudden death of her husband. It helped open my eyes to a dangerous pattern within families that I see being repeated.

Cousin Etta abruptly sold her gorgeous furniture, gave away valuable family treasures and left her upscale Manhattan apartment to live with her son. Later, she moved to the Midwest to live in a flat to be near my mother, her first cousin. Within a few months, she packed up her remaining things and quietly moved to California to be near her sister.

On the last leg of her sojourn, Etta moved back to New York to an unfurnished, public housing studio apartment. She was down to three pieces of luggage and a footlocker trunk. She gave up every possession she held dear in search of a nest that could never be again.

After Cousin Etta's son had a fatal heart attack, she was too weary to cry; she could only moan. Etta died shortly thereafter, refusing to approve a minor surgical procedure because, as she told me, she couldn't think of one good reason to live.

As she firmly held me, her baby cousin, in her long arms for what we both knew would be the last time, she showed me what bravery is all about.

It was on her own terms that she made the choice to return to dust. She was secure of her place in the eternal and she was anxious to go.

I trembled in the face of her firm commitment to be free. She was as determined to die as a newborn is to live. Her final appointment came with clear thinking. Her emotional bags were packed and she was prepared to leave this earth. It was I who was reluctant to let her go. But then you understand it and accept it. Three days later, Etta died.

As I sat alone with her body in an anteroom, near the main funeral parlor chapel, I combed her hair the way she would have preferred and wiped lipstick from her thin lips. It was the last thing any loved one could do for her final public appearance. Her last choice — to die — was her last, successful attempt to find a nest reminiscent of home.

I still struggle with the heartache I felt about the end of Cousin Etta's life. During her last three years, I witnessed the steady disintegration of her world. Though her decline was gradual, I can only pray that her ascension from her earthly coil was swift and beautiful. All I know for certain is that she welcomed the transition.

Some of the things Etta went through instruct my life. Since she abruptly uprooted and constantly moved, she destroyed her support system. The familiar infrastructure was no longer there to soothe her as it should have been.

As an unknown elderly woman in a new environment, she spent all of her days and nights alone. Except for our morning and bedtime phone calls, and occasional visits, she was left to face life, alone.

Of course guilt is always about you, not the other person. But I regret not speaking up when Etta said she wanted to change her life and move to another town. My lack of experience in giving advice to family members consigned me to the role of the child.

In the pecking order of my family members, I held a lowly position. Being the baby of my immediate family, I was accustomed to asking for advice rather than giving it. It took awhile to step into the role of mature adult with ideas and opinions worth listening to.

There was an almost noticeable shifting of positions between Etta and me. I was a woman with enough seasoning to be taken seriously by a family matriarch. My role was as new to me as hers was as a widow. We could have been a better team. I never knew that a woman could die from a broken heart or that a life could end so unnoticed.

Once Etta embraced death, she had a peacefulness that had been absent most of her life. Mourning a severely broken heart is a lengthy process. When it doesn't run its normal course, the remaining pain can consume the spirit we need to live.

In an attempt to learn from the past and to become more sensitive, my sister and I are working on improving our care-giving skills. Our goal is to be better daughters to our aging mother. We are actively involved in discussions and decisions that affect the quality of our mother's life.

Our hearts break a little at a time as we watch our mother struggle to get up from a chair or put on her shoes that are too tight because of swollen ankles. We wait patiently for her to descend several stairs, with her hand firmly clutching her cane. We weep inwardly for the days gone by, when mother dashed around with the energy and grace of a dancer.

We can only guarantee that the rest of her life will be a collaborative effort on our part, as well as hers. No matter how much she complains about us meddling in her business, we know it's just overflowing heartaches and pain. She has outlived everyone that she can remember from her past life.

## A Lovers' Love Lost

Your heart can hurt in many different chambers.

When Marjorie was 53, her husband of thirty years deserted her for one of his office interns. The 22-year-old intern was pregnant with his child.

There is never a good time to get bad news. Marjorie's life was already chaotic because of the lavish wedding she and her husband were planning for their only child. The daughter's wedding had been planned for a year and the two stressful events happened almost simultaneously.

Because of the ugly circumstances of the marital split up, her daughter and future son-in-law jumped at the chance to move. They moved to the new son-in-law's hometown of Gary, Indiana.

Jackie, Marjorie's daughter, literally ran away as soon as possible after her wedding. Her father's affair created a terrible climate before her wedding and the promise of a new life. When her father's baby was born, Jackie's marriage license, Marjorie's divorce decree and the baby's birth certificate were all signed about the same time.

Although the ex-husband did not marry his young lover, the indiscretion of the affair and the birth of the child left Marjorie deeply wounded. She felt abandoned by her daughter and husband. Marjorie was heartbroken.

Marjorie seemed to grow old, overnight. Her once long, graceful body looked shorter and thicker. Her footsteps became heavy as she moved methodically through her daily office routines. Although, she managed to perform competently in her professional life, she was becoming another person.

Silently, Marjorie was grieving and racked with pain. Losing a daughter to marriage and her husband to another woman more than half her age, left a void in Marjorie that work could not fill.

Initially Marjorie's friends and co-workers strongly supported her as she endured a bitter divorce. But in her conversations, Marjorie couldn't move past her victimization and pain. Her constant tears and anger soon wore down most of her supporters.

After awhile, many of Marjorie's associates avoided her. The ongoing drama of her situation became the stuff of office gossip. Marjorie's rants became therapy to vent about her devastation. However, she still took the pain home, every night.

For some reason, mature women feel worse if their divorce or break up is due to a younger woman. There is an irrational fear on the part of mature women that they will be displaced by youth.

Unfortunately, our culture causes mature women to feel bad about themselves, during a divorce. We shouldn't, but many of us take a man's life-crisis situation as if it were our problem. Stop taking ownership of a man's mid-life crisis that you neither created nor control.

Marjorie fell into a predictable low self-esteem pattern. She fed herself with anger to mask her embarrassment about how her husband left her. She began to regularly berate most of the men she encountered. Like many women that I've known, Marjorie spent her time and energy painting the worse pictures possible of her ex. She occasionally got the attention she craved as a result of her male bashing, from other equally miserable women.

However, demonstrating open anger for men gets nothing accomplished, except isolating oneself. Anger is an anti-social and self-destructive emotion. In its battle against natural harmony, anger seeks to disturb the order of the universe. Anger feeds conflict and conflict destroys peace.

Like many people who whine and complain, Marjorie found herself excluded from gatherings where people wanted to have a good time. She was left alone with her fear that was masked by her acting out toward men. That was the symptom. She hated the feeling she harbored of not being able to compete for her husband and win. That was her culprit, not men.

## It's Really Over

Many unmarried and previously married, mature women find themselves in Marjorie's emotional state — brokenhearted and angry because of years wasted in a relationship that shocked them by the suddenness and cruelty of its ending. The feeling of lost time is ever present for women who spent precious years in their 30s or 40s in failed relationships.

Understanding the reasons for failed relationships is important, but the bottom line is that there is a lasting residue of pain, especially when you're 45 and beyond.

Reaching the age of 50 is a human milestone, but lost love is no different at any age. However, being past 45 pushes a feeling of despair with which youth does not have to cope. Time becomes precious. Healing will take more time. We all suffer in our own fashion, but at some point we have to let it go and open ourselves for new love.

## Help is Near

Although we may hide behind the blackest veil, upheaval finds us and, to put it indelicately, shit happens. Collecting the pieces and putting them back together is hard work not meant for wimps.

It's a messy business and nowhere is that clearer than when you see friends in crisis. If we are truly friends, we feel responsible for nurturing them until they are whole, again. While it is true that demonstrating compassion for wounded friends is time-consuming and inconvenient, true friendship is neither inconvenienced nor is it insensitive.

Maintaining contact by phone, e-mail or personal notes can be ways to stay in touch with a friend until you can visit. The positive side of routine social events is that as human beings, we find a calm in regularly looking forward to something. It gives us something for which to live.

It is easy to set up a lunch date with friends the first Friday of every month or attend a spa on a regular day of the week. You could arrange to meet after church to chat or schedule a card party or book club once a month at your home. Anything that encourages positive interaction with other people is a way for all of us to feel connected.

Some of us are more resilient than others. If we are genuinely strong within ourselves, then we can accept fragile friends who need to be included in situations that nurture and promote self-confidence.

How many of us, as shy children, found great companionship with other children who were bolder and less fearful of the world? You bonded because someone who was your opposite pulled you into doing things and going places you never would on your on.

It is true that we change with age, but our personalities, formed at a young age, rarely change in drastic ways.

## Protecting Yourself

Friends and family can be supportive when we are hurt by failed relationships. But at our age, we must be smarter in love than we were at twenty-five or thirty-five. Time is definitely not on our side and we must protect ourselves and depend on "common sense" that is a lifetime in the making.

Opening your heart and getting back in the game of love is scary. If you are afraid your openness may be used as a bull's-eye, here are some survival tips for navigating the treacherous waters of relationships.

There are stages that all relationships go through that will tell you if you are going to have a pleasure trip or a bumpy ride. Pay attention and be ready to make changes to protect yourself, if necessary.

## The Affair Stage

### The beginning — You meet Mr. WSM (wonderfully seasoned man)

The honeymoon period is always fast, furious and off the hook. It is a smorgasbord of new adventures, frequent sex, dinners and phone calls. This stage can be as brief as a week or as long as three months but, inevitably, it will settle down.

It's what's left after the honeymoon smoke clears that will determine if this incredible affair with WSM will segue way into a meaningful, mutually satisfying relationship. Seasoned relationships happen quickly. Both players know the game.

Within the first four to six months, you'll have a good idea whether your man has the potential to be a long-term lover. Does he call you spontaneously or is he locked into speaking to you on certain days of the week and always at the same time of day?

Does he indicate a future introduction to his family and friends? Does he go out of his way to please you? Does he cancel prior commitments to be there for you? Does he make you happy?

## The Relationship Stage
### The middle — after six months

If the romance light is green and you're ready to merge with traffic, ignore the honking horn behind you and give yourself a chance to empty your vehicle of the debris leftover from your previous relationship.

Give him a chance to do the same. He had a life before he met you and there was a woman in it, somewhere. If you find that you had a relationship in need of closure, be careful. This is a crucial stage in your new relationship where honesty and trust will be put to the test.

Once you both acknowledge that there are people still in your lives even though you are involved with each other, you have taken a giant step toward deciding what kind of relationship you will have.

If there are no significant others, then you have a free rein to explore each other. This is the pivotal period for falling in love or walking away without feeling too foolish.

Ignoring what your family and friends think (this is your life, after all), make an honest assessment of your new man. Is this the man you could love? Allow your common sense to lead you where your instinct is pointing.

Trust your gut feelings. If you don't feel it's right deep down, you can still break it off without either of you getting hurt too much. The faith in your decision to stay will push you closer together.

## Resolution
### Final Stage — within the year
After seasoned men and seasoned women experience a year or more of enjoyment from a positive relationship, usually the living arrangements change. Forget about long engagements or marriages that take years of planning. Because time is so precious, seasoned couples usually marry quickly.

## Caution — Heartbreak Ahead
### Still stuck in the honeymoon stage
If the new seasoned man in your life exhibits little or none of the actions spelled out in the stages-of-a-relationship sequence, cut him loose or — less drastic — put him on a maintenance program.

If you remain together for four to six months and the two of you are not demonstrating reciprocal supportive behaviors leading to a closer relationship, start pulling back — especially if you have shown great affection and feel used by being overly considerate.

After six months, you will know if you have a relationship in the making or not. It is a defining point to either dig in and stay or get your hat and leave.

The key factor here is that each of you makes an equal effort to be together. When a man wants you, his behavior makes his intentions clear. His behavior will mirror his talk and not oppose it.

Walking away is easier than waiting for him to leave you. Another reality is that it is possible for a good man and a good woman to fight for the chance to have a relationship, and fail.

If you love the man, you will be heartbroken when the relationship is over. The circumstances will not matter. You feel pain, loss and some anger. You may not be as angry as Marjorie, who after a lifetime of marriage had to rebuild her life, but you'll have your share. It is essential to move on with your life, and put the broken heart back together, again.

## Fill Up the Cracks in Your Heart
### Get Busy

You should start seeing other men and continue to see him occasionally, if you wish and at your pleasure. You can put him on your schedule, but do not accommodate him by granting him special time.

Meet him for lunch instead of dinner and for daytime events, insist that they be in public. This arrangement allows you to have male companionship as you look further. If you have a busy social life, you won't feel so empty.

Do not cut off all ties to him, if you really care for him. Keep him user-friendly in the maintenance program. But make it clear that you are no longer available to him, exclusively. Have sex if sex is what you need or want from him. If he accepts a lesser role in your life, his power over you will diminish because of his weaker position. Learn to enjoy what you like of him. Empower yourself to have options.

Your self-image and healing will increase once you feel more equal to the value you have given him. If you were heartbroken because you felt victimized, then my suggestions will help mend your heart and make it whole, again.

Reconnect with wonderful men you used to work with or knew socially, even if you're not interested in them romantically. All women should have a cadre of wonderful men companions. Platonic male friends keep your spirits up. They listen well and seldom add drama to your life.

Accept dates from decent, hard-working men that you avoided because you thought you were too good, too tall or too educated for them. Some of the most wonderful men will never make People's "Fifty Sexiest Men," but they can be great companions.

Lower your nose to fall in love with a "nice" man, maybe even a nerd. If you were jerked around by a wonderfully seasoned man, WSM, try dating a decent regular guy. Women gravitate to smooth, selfish men and regularly pass up the nice guys. Do something good for your heart and heal with a man that seriously wants to be with you.

Be up front. Tell the next man you get involved with what you're looking for in a relationship. He'll stay if he's interested and if not, it's time saved.

## Repairs to the Heart

Aging makes us feel vulnerable in all areas. But nothing is more fragile than the heart. Years of loving and losing have left broken pieces all over the landscape of our lives. To continue each day, we need the concern and caring of our community, friends and family to replenish us.

The chance to connect and move on with our lives is the passion of the journey. The heart is where passion lives. A whole heart is one that houses healthy passion. A healthy heart must be protected and treated with wholesome respect, if it is going to endure and go the distance.

The death of loved ones and the death of lost love leaves intolerable scars. But there is always the hope that heals, the hope that promises the birth of a grandchild or the birth of a new love. Hope is timeless and it is ageless.

# Kicking the Recipe Across the Table
## Cracks in the Heart

1. Does the worst pain in your life no longer hurt like it once did?

2. What did it take to heal after the death of a parent or husband?

3. Has the pain from a lost love made you bitter?

4. Are failed relationships harder to get over than the death of a loved one?

5. Is it possible to be hurt so deeply that you never recover?

6. What effective techniques do you use to heal yourself?

7. Does getting older lessen the hurt of loss?

# Sources Consulted

Balch, James F. and Balch, Phyllis A. <u>Prescription for Nutritional Healing</u>, 2d ed. New York: Avery Publishing Group, 1997.

Bonvillain, Nancy. <u>Language, Culture and Communication: The Meaning of Messages</u>. Englewood Cliffs: Prentice-Hall, Inc., 1993.

Borisoff, Deborah and Merrill, Lisa. <u>The Power to Communicate</u>. Prospect Heights, Illinois: Waveland Press, Inc., 1987.

Casale, Brenda. *"Everything You Always Wanted to Know About Cosmetic Surgery, But Were Afraid to Ask."* Washington, D.C., AARP/Modern Maturity magazine, March/April, 2001.

Dates, Jannette and Barlow, William, ed. <u>Split Image: African Americans in the Media</u>. Washington, D.C.: Howard University Press, 1990.

Hall, Edward T. <u>The Silent Language</u>. Greenwich, Conn: Fawcett Publications, Inc. 1959.

Hall, Edward T. <u>Beyond Culture</u>. Garden City, New York: Anchor Press/Doubleday, 1977.

<u>Holy Bible, King James Version</u>. Camden New Jersey: Thomas Nelson, 1972.

**Faludi, Susan.** Backlash: The Undeclared War Against American Women. New York: Doubleday, 1992.

**Goldhaber, Gerald, M.** Organizational Communication, 2d ed. Dubuque, Iowa: William C. Brown Company, Publishers, 1974.

Culture, Society and the Media. Ed. Michael Gurevitch, Tony Bennett, James Curran and Janet Woollcott. London and New York: Routledge, 1995.

**Head, Palmer, T.** *"Subordinates' Perception of Androgynous Communication Style of Black Female Managers, As a Factor in Subordinates' Job Satisfaction"* Ph.D. dissertation, Howard University, 1986.

**Loehle, Craig.** Thinking Strategically. Cambridge: Cambridge University Press, 1996.

**Mindell, Phyllis.** A Woman's Guide to the Language of Success. Paramus, New Jersey: Prentice Hall, 1996.

**Pogrebin, Letty Cottin.** Getting Over Getting Older, An Intimate Journey. New York: Berkley Books, 1997.

**Russel, Cheryl.** Racial and Ethnic Diversity. New York: New Strategic Publications, Inc. 1996.

**Scanzoni, John H.** Sex Roles, Lifestyles and Childbearing. New York: The Free Press, 1975.

**Sheehy, Gail.** <u>New Passages, Mapping Your Life Across Time</u>. New York: Random House, 1995.

**Steiner, George A.** <u>Strategic Planning: What Every Manager Must Know</u>. New York: Free Press Paperbacks, 1979.

**The Boston Women's Health Book Collective.** <u>Our Bodies, Our Selves</u>. New York: Simon and Schuster, 1992.

**United States Government Printing Office.** *"Living Arrangements Report"* Washington, D.C.: Bureau of Census, 1994, 2001.

**Willis, Mary.** *"Eyes Wide Shut."* AARP/Modern Maturity magazine. Washington D.C.: March/April, 2001.

# About the Author

Theda Palmer Saxton, Ph.D., is an Interpersonal Communications Practioner. She lives with her husband Bill, a professional musician, on the Upper West Side of Manhattan and she has a son, Anthony.

She is well known for her seminars and workshops for organizations seeking to improve communications. Her private client base of women and their families, in personal communication crisis situations, continues to grow.

Dr. Palmer Saxton is a life coach for those who know her best.

## Cover Artist

Will Saxton, native New Yorker, has been creating fluid visual images of deep spiritual moods, with overtones of the social issues of the day, for over ten years. His keen eye for detail captures the moment and preserves it.

*Will exhibits his work frequently and is the son of Harlem born, jazz great, Bill Saxton.*